Thou Art With Me

May comfort and hope be attained by all who read

Thou Art With Me:

Passing On of Companions

❧〜❦

May the Lord's blessings rest upon this publication.   We pray those blessings will be multiplied as the stories in this book are read and shared.

Thou Art With Me

Passing On of Companions

ANNA MARY ZIMMERMAN, EDITOR
ROY B. ZIMMERMAN, PUBLISHER

ROANN MENNONITE PUBLISHERS
22425 C.R. 42
GOSHEN, IN 46526-9215

For Thou Art With Me—Passing On of Companions

ISBN: 0-9665661-0-6

ROANN MENNONITE PUBLISHERS
22425 CR 42
Goshen, IN 46526-9215

Printed by The Print Place, Shipshewana, Indiana.
Printed in the USA.

Contents

———— ❧❧ ————

The cross is for life; the crown is for eternity.

Preface

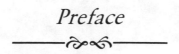

"But the God of all grace, who hath called us unto his eternal glory by Christ Jesus, after that ye have suffered a while, make you perfect, stablish, strengthen, settle you" (I Peter 5:10).

God has called us into an "extended family" of those with whom we share a common bond: the loss of our loved ones.

Our family's experience with death was the sudden loss of three of our children on two different occasions. We also lost a granddaughter to sudden death on another occasion.

Over the years we have learned that healing comes in various ways. One way that has been a blessing to us is to reach out to others who have suffered the loss of family members.

We attended a meeting on "Coping With Grief" in 1998 in the state of Pennsylvania. There we met many men and women whose bosom companions had been called out of this life. Several of these lonely ones suggested we print their stories for them. That is how the idea of this book, *Thou Art With Me*, was born.

Out of love, and with compassion for others, the families wanted to tell their stories. For in the telling, there is healing. However, the *process* of telling is not always easy.

One whom has suffered mental anguish following her husband's death shares: *"This has been very difficult for me to write, knowing I am baring my innermost struggles, but I do this with the thought, if just one person can find comfort in knowing they are not alone, and can get the help they need, it will be worth it all. There is light ahead and God's comfort is ever-present in the storm."*

Another contributor wrote: *"When God calls to Himself a husband, making that husband's wife a widow, He is placing a difficult calling into her hands. I won't pretend it's not hard, and God Himself knows just how hard it is. I can see how well He knows when I see the emphasis in His word on being a support to widows. We often say we only realize the value of something when we lose it. Having been the wife of a husband, I can say that's true even in a marriage."*

We trust *Thou Art With Me* will help many who are going through the process of grieving and healing. One has expressed it so well: *"We don't face a blank wall where we have no hope of being with our loved one again. Neither is it an open door for us to go through, but it is a window where we can catch glimpses of the glory awaiting us."*

When it comes to the landscape of grief and sorrow, there's no better guide than someone who's been there. But even the guide may need a guide.

You may not yet find comfort in reading of the experiences of others—it may be too soon. If so, put the book aside for a while and come back to it later.

May each one trust God who is the source of all our hope and faith.

-amz

Other books in print by Roann Mennonite Publishers:

He Restoreth My Soul: Personal Stories of Sudden Loss
Book One. ISBN: 0-9665661-1-4

He Restoreth My Soul: Personal Stories of Sudden Loss
Book Two. ISBN: 0-9665661-2-2

Be strong and of a good courage;
be not afraid, neither be thou dismayed:
for the Lord thy God is with thee
whithersoever thou goest.

Joshua 1:9b

We feel greatly indebted to all who graciously contributed their stories to *Thou Art With Me;* also to Naomi Ramer for her assistance and advice as proofreader.

Roann Mennonite Publishers
Anna Mary Zimmerman, Editor
Roy B. Zimmerman, Publisher

The Path Leads Home
By: One Who Has Been There

I met my companion at a place where two ways joined into one. Being delighted with our friendship and enjoying the pleasantness of mutual sharing, we agreed to travel together. We both felt it was the path God was leading us to tread, and we rejoiced in His goodness.

And so we began our journey together, hand-in-hand, enjoying the pleasant scenery, and content with our lot. We had no worries or sighs for the future, for does not the path lead home? All the world seemed new and fresh, there was not a cloud in the sky, the sun shone brightly, and the path stretching ahead appeared level and smooth. Blessings seemed enhanced and trials lessened as we shared together this pathway of life. We strengthened our mutual determination to always follow the right path, for it had been trod by the Son of God himself, and it was the path to home. And so we two went on together.

At times on the way, there were sudden dips or turns, but we knew that we could not expect the way to always be easy, or to have continual sunshine. We knew that the way may be rough and steep, and beset by sorrow and care, yet it leads home. And we knew that heaven will surely be worth it all. Then too, we had each other to lean on, and no path seemed so difficult as to render our mutual faith and strength ineffectual. If the way was not always easy, at least it was clearly marked, and so we two went on together.

By degrees, almost imperceptibly, the path grew more rough and began trending downward. My companion found her strength lessening under the rigors of these new difficulties. I wished for a smoother way, for it seemed to me not fair that her strength should be less, and the path harder for her than for others. But with wonderful patience she traveled on, and complained but seldom, and bore her part bravely. We found comfort and strength in our God, and felt His good hand upon us, to be with us and lead us home. And so we went on together.

The path then took a very unexpected turn, and we halted for a moment in utter disbelief. Before us was a more dismal scene than we could have imagined, and made all former difficulties seem insignificant by its breadth and scope. Ahead of us for a long way stretched a bleak and cheerless valley, the depths of which were covered by a mist which shadowed and concealed the path we were to take. The air was more chilly here, for the chasm was too deep to catch many of the Son's rays. Through the mist we could hear the sullen turbulence of a river, as it rolled unseen beneath the gloom. We turned and looked at each other, then at the darksome prospect ahead. I felt a shiver of apprehension as we gathered our courage and strength for the greatest test we had ever faced. We called upon our God, and spoke encouraging words together, but I dreaded the journey. I knew that my companion was not so strong as before, and this way was so rough and steep, and I feared greatly lest I lose her in this place. Yes, this was the right path, the one that would lead us home, but why must it traverse this dark and dreaded place? However dark it may seem, we knew that His grace was sufficient, and so we encouraged ourselves in the Lord, and went on together.

Then feeling something of grim optimism, we descended into the abyss and were wrapt in the enshrouding gloom. Yes, we would fain have chosen an easier way, but time urged us onward, and we knew that to regain the heights beyond, we must travel the way before us, howe'er rough and steep it may be. I was sore distressed for my companion's sake, for the way was hard and her strength greatly lessened. I bade her to lean on me for it was very rough here, and dark, for the mist shadowed all and made it hard to see. I desperately wished to escape this place, and had continual dread of losing my beloved companion in this strange and awful valley, for she was greatly weakened and the journey seemed too great for her. But still we two went on together.

Presently the air grew yet more chill and damp, and darkness seemed to be closing in. The path, too, seemed rougher and less defined, when suddenly my companion slipped from my grasp and in a moment was gone. Oh, the loneliness and anguish of that parting. I felt as if part of me had been torn away, and the pain seemed unbearable. In agony I stumbled forward a few feet further and saw in the blackness a mighty river; turgid, restless, and deep. I knew then that this place was the valley and shadow of death and that here at my feet rolled the river Jordan. Overcome by grief at my loss, and the loneliness of the future, I fell onto the bank of the river and wept until it seemed I could weep no more. I poured out my heart to my God and He listened with a heart of love and understanding. He brought such comfort to me as would sooth my soul and heal my wounds. In memory I traveled back on the path we had taken together. It seemed such a short time ago that we had shared this pathway, and even in her weakness she had helped and strengthened me, and added meaning to my life. Now she was gone and I must walk alone.

Finally, with great effort I rose to my feet and considered my state. I was greatly weakened, I had no helpmeet, I was in the depths of a great valley, and the way ahead seemed more than I could bear. Compelled by time, I moved away from the river's edge, and slowly, oh so slowly, began this journey. At first I had but little strength, which seemed to be easily expended in grief. I wandered in numbed loneliness, for it seemed no joy to walk alone, and in such a place. The way, for the first while, seemed rougher and harder than any I had been on before. But for the helping hand of my God, I should have perished in the depths of that valley. I longed for her presence beside me to encourage and aid me, to add her strength and prayers to mine, to cheer and brighten the way. Though I missed her sorely, yet I knew that she had safely crossed over Jordan, that her weakness and pain were gone, that unpleasant shadows and hard paths would befall her no more. I longed to join her and rejoice in bliss together, but none can cross Jordan in his own strength, or choose the time of his crossing. Though I grieved sorely, yet I found no small solace in my God, for He did comfort me, His heart was touched with my grief.

After what seemed like a long while, the path began to trend upward, became less treacherous and more defined, the mists less dense, the air lighter and warmer. Occasionally the path would rise above the mist, and I would look back in wonder over that dark valley. With a certain pang I could even see the path that we had taken as we entered, and it seemed but a short time ago that we were together at that place. As I look back over the forbidding scene, I am more sure than ever that only by God's help did I make it through. I turned to go up the path once more, scarce believing that I had passed through such a valley, yet believing when I saw that I walked alone. Though it may not always be an easy journey, yet it seems to grow easier with the passing of time. I am sure too that she is there waiting for me, cheering me on, and rejoicing in my Homeward progress. I seem to hear her say, "Yes, heaven surely is worth it all!" And then I am more certain than ever that the path leads home.

-Anonymous

EARL W. OBERHOLTZER
October 15, 1948 to June 13, 1975 (26 years)

MARK W. OBERHOLTZER
January 25, 1958 to June 13, 1975 (17 years)

A Double Call
Erla Oberholtzer, Wife & Sister-In-Law

It was a beautiful sunny day June 13, 1975. The morning began very peaceful and relaxed, in fact so relaxed that we overslept! Chores were begun as usual and neither of us seemed to mind being late. Had I known what God had in store for us yet that day I might not have enjoyed the quiet morning as I was now.

We lived on a dairy farm and working with my husband was a pleasure. Chore time was a relaxing time for me. Of course, being the parents of four healthy children, there were times we were kept quite busy. As a mother knows, these were busy but happy days. The children were always anxious to go along out to the barn. They would play with their tricycles or else watch their mom and daddy milk cows and chore.

The day went on. There was lots to do as we had intentions to go pick strawberries in the evening. So I tried to finish some Saturday jobs. Daddy took the older children along to the feed mill in the morning, so I got my laundry done, plus some cleaning. Dinner was a happy meal. We all enjoyed our morning and each of the children had lots to tell Mom.

It didn't seem long till we heard Uncle Mark in the field lane with the tractor. Plans were to haul manure from the calf pit in the afternoon.

Earl looked at me and said, "Well, I guess I must go." As I look back now, he seemed rather reluctant to leave. Did he sense our time together was short? He went outside and I put our little ones down for naps and then went outside to mow lawn.

I came in to check the children some time later and then Earl also came in for a drink. He looked at me and said, "My, you look like you're warm. You really don't need to do all that today, do you?" No, the mowing didn't really all have to be done that day. But as I said, it was such a nice day and I really felt like doing it. This was the last time Earl was inside the house.

After the children woke up from their naps we went outside. While I was washing our car, both Earl and Mark came to the front of the barn. They needed some tools from the workbench. Earl told me they were having a problem with the manure pump. He dropped a wrench, and now a nut, into the pit. He was calmly telling me about it and didn't seem at all concerned.

At the same time Mark was playing with the children. He was tossing the children in the air, while asking if I wanted to wash his car, too. I told him I didn't know if I could do it good enough for a teenager.

About this time the children got into a dispute over something and Daddy told them, "Stop your fighting." These were the last words I heard Earl say.

It was soon time to get the barn ready for evening milking, one of my normal chores. While I was outside, I went to check if Earl would soon be coming for supper. As I walked out back the tractor was running and no one was around. On top of the pit, side-by-side lay a cap and a straw hat. This drew my attention. With an abnormal feeling I walked over and looked into the pit. Was something preparing me for the shock I was about to receive?

I saw Earl laying on his side at the bottom of the pit. I called his name a few times and didn't get a response. So I ran to the barn to call for help. I then went and called our children. They must have sensed there was something serious I wanted to talk about, for they came quickly.

I sat down with them around me and told them what I really hadn't fathomed yet myself. I said, "I think your daddy just died." They looked at me with big questioning eyes. "What happened?" I tried my best to explain, but this was my first of many explanations time and time again.

It was about this time I heard my father-in-law coming and I went back to the pit again after telling the children to stay in front of the barn. It was then that I saw Mark also laying on his back at the bottom of the pit—two brothers laying side-by-side in death. Things moved on rapidly from here on. But I was given strength when and where it was needed. Yes, we do have a merciful God!

I had never seen the rope Mark had tied to Earl's arm, letting one end lie at the top of the pit. He tried his best to save his brother's life, but laid down his own life trying to save his brother. Apparently as they were working at the top of the pit, methane gas fumes had overtaken Earl and he fell into the pit. Mark tried to rescue his brother and was also overtaken with fumes. This was only 20 to 30 minutes after the time we last talked together.

I often had to marvel how God allowed me to see only what he felt was enough at one time. I even was given strength to help lift my husband out of that dark pit. And surely anyone knows I could not have done that on my own.

By this time family, friends, neighbors, ambulances, and policemen were arriving at our farm. For a long time after this, my children were fearful of sirens. If we'd meet up with an ambulance they'd ask, "Mama, what happened now?" I was often thankful for the neighbor lady who stayed with me till my family arrived. I don't remember what we talked about, but just having someone there meant so much.

I was just in a state of shock. My mind felt numb and I could not even cry. It took a few hours until things finally made sense and reality took hold.

The next few days were just a blur to me. We traveled onward by God's strength and the prayers of our loved ones.

There were one thousand people at the viewing and many more than a church full of people at the double funeral. I remember thinking if so many people care and are praying for us, surely we can go on.

Shortly after the funeral my father-in-law came to try to encourage me. He gave me some very good advice by telling me to "try and keep family life as normal as possible." "You are now the head of the family. Read to the children as you always did." Had he sensed that it was hard for me just then to try be a Father as well as a Mother to my children? I don't know, but it was just what I needed right then.

It was two-and-one-half months later when our dear little daughter was born. She was healthy and added joy to our family. (Joy in the 'midst of sorrow.) One of my first thoughts as I held her in my arms were, "The Lord has given and the Lord has taken away, blessed be the name of the Lord." Job's words also came to my mind while I was sitting there waiting for help with my family, *"Not my will but thine be done."*

I was now a widow with five preschool children to love and care for. My biggest concern was, I wanted to keep my family together.

My family grew up so fast. We made plenty of mistakes, and still do, but with God's help we'll try to follow the path He has laid out for each of us. Though the path be thorny and full of rocks at times, we will continue on knowing and trusting in His promises: "I will never leave thee nor forsake thee."

There always seemed to be decisions to make, which has a way to wear one down, but I often found as one door closes another one opens—if only I have patience to wait on the Lord.

Only my two oldest children really remember their dad. This was hard for me to accept, as they were all close to Dad. But a very young child's mind can't hold on to memories, and can accept changes rather quickly. But that does not take away the fact that our family is different.

"Why did God take our dad?" was a question often asked. Giving an answer to such a question is not easy.

I knew as they grew up, the children often felt a void which I could not fill. I tried, but must confess I often failed.

God's mercies are new every morning. I have so much to be thankful for. As the children grew to maturity they seemed to realize life is real, and God has a purpose for them in life, too.

My children were all blessed with Christian companions of their own and are all blessed with children to raise. My prayer is that God will grant them wisdom to raise these "jewels" for Him, for they are a real joy to me.

God has been so good to us! We know not what the future holds, but we know Who holds the future.

—*Erla Oberholtzer*
Denver, Pennsylvania

"He healeth the broken in heart, and bindeth up their wounds" (Psalm 147:3).

ERVIN MARTIN
October 27, 1941 to January 9, 1999 (57 years)

Crossing The Valley
Elvina Martin, Wife

On a cold winter's day, Wednesday, December 23, 1998, after telling everyone good-by, Ervin and I were leaving home to go to St. Mary's Hospital. He was scheduled for surgery at 9:00 that morning.

Ervin had a cancerous tumor in his esophagus which the doctors wanted to remove. To do this they had to break two ribs and collapse one lung to get to the area where they wanted to work. We were told over and over that this is a very major surgery. We tried to prepare ourselves for the worst. Prayers were needed, but we always tried to say *"Thy will be done."*

Ten minutes before 9:00 the orderly came with the stretcher. "Are you ready, Mr. Martin?" was the call that came through the door? He was moved to the stretcher, smiled once more, and with a good-by, he was gone.

Our son and daughter-in-law came to stay with me as we knew that it would be a long wait. We were ushered to a waiting room where we waited for two hours and fifty minutes till a doctor came and informed us all went well. They had to take out one-fourth of his stomach to get all the cancer cells. We waited another hour while he was in recovery before we could see him. Then we went to the intensive care ward where we were told we could see him. When we got up there, we were told to just wait another half-an-hour as they were not ready for us to see Ervin. That was a long tense wait.

When we came back to the desk again and asked if we could see Mr. Martin now, they let us in. We had been told before that Ervin would probably have a breathing machine, or life support, for one or two days. At least we were partly prepared to see all those tubes and machines fastened to him. But I had never seen anyone on life support before, so it looked kind of frightening. Visiting was nil because of the big tube in his throat.

Ervin needed the life support only one day, then he was on his own. He had a pain pump strapped to his hand that he could use every seven minutes for the first few days. Then he was put on the needle.

Each day we saw a change for the better.

Friday, December 25, 1998, he was sitting in a chair for ten minutes.

By Sunday, December 27, he already was starting to walk a little with the help of nurses. Each day he walked a little more. Also his diet changed to Jell-O and juices instead of just intravenous feeding and it seemed to agree with him.

Wednesday, December 30, the nurses sent us out into the hall to walk him alone. I carried Ervin's drain bag and pushed his I-V pole along. It seemed to go well under his condition. When we came back to his room the nurses said, "If he keeps this up, he can go home shortly." That evening he had a meal of mashed potatoes, creamed corn, and gravy which tasted good to him.

Thursday, December 31, the day before New Year's Day, things started to change. He ran a high fever and was shorter in breath. He already had oxygen full-time, but it just didn't seem to help anymore.

Friday, January 1, 1999, his brother came to see him after supper. The nurses were there in a hurry and said, "No visitors. Mr. Martin is a very sick man."

Then things started to change in my mind. His one leg began to swell. The doctors called it a blood clot and added more tubes to try and dissolve it. His abdomen started to fill with fluid (infection they called it). Another tube was put in but to no avail. It didn't drain.

Saturday, January 2, they took Ervin to surgery and removed old, dried blood the size of two fists. But things still didn't change for the better. He still had a high fever.

Tuesday, January 5, they used a big needle to try and remove fluid from his back, but couldn't get to the right spot.

Thursday, January 7, they also suspected a blood clot in Ervin's lung, so they took him to the pulmonary section to check him, then to CAT scan to see if they could remove more fluid under x-ray. The doctors said they got a little but not what they had hoped for. That all made Ervin very weak. Then they took him to recovery. While in recovery he stopped breathing, so they put him on life-support again. It was another four hours before we could see him again.

I asked the doctor, "Would it be wise to get our family together as we'd like to be together once more." He said we may start calling them right away. We have a family of eleven children, six are married, so it took a while to all get to the hospital.

I had spent the last two nights in the hospital so I felt kind of worn out. Our family was all together for about two hours, then it looked like things might stay stable. So the children went home to their families, and my sister and brother-in-law came to stay with me, waiting to see what the morning holds for us.

Friday, January 8, I asked how long we should leave life-support on if the doctors don't think he can get well. So in the afternoon I got the family and the doctor together again. The doctor explained very nicely to us that all his medications just didn't seem to take hold. They were up against and had tried all they could. But they had changed medication one more time and wanted to wait to see how he would be in the morning. At one time I counted nine bags attached to him.

The next morning, Saturday, January 9, things looked no better. Our children and deacon were called to come help us make decisions.

When the children were all together again, the doctor came and explained Ervin's condition to us. At the most, he could live only 24 hours with life-support. If they turned it off, it would only be half-an-hour or so until he would die. The nurses asked if we'd like to sing a few songs for him yet. So we sang "What A Friend We Have In Jesus" and a few others. I often wonder if he still heard us.

Shortly after that, the minister dropped in yet, too. We had a prayer together. Oh! What a comfort... Then I recognized that fluid (infection) was running out of Ervin's mouth. Talking things over with the family, it was decided we were just lengthening his life in pain with the machine. So we gave the nurses consent to turn it off. It was a hard thing to do, but we saw he was living in misery. I said, *"Lord, Thy will be done."*

It took two hours till they had the machine turned down altogether, as the nurses did it very slowly. When the machine was turned off, they gave Ervin oxygen through a mask yet. He lived half-an-hour on his own before he passed on to his reward. We could all be in his room until the Lord called him home.

We asked the nurses if we could see Ervin with all the tubes off yet before we go home. That left nice memories to leave the hospital and see him resting so peacefully after such a struggle for life.

We passed through a heavy snowfall to a home that would never be the same again. But we want to be thankful we have those everlasting arms to lean on for support.

May God richly bless each one!

—*Elvina Martin*
West Montrose, Ontario, Canada

"The eternal God is thy refuge, and underneath are the everlasting arms: and he shall thrust out the enemy from before thee; (Deuteronomy 33:27).

EARL H. MARTIN
December 12, 1944 to April 2, 1997 (52 years)

Behold, The Hand Of God
Mary H. Martin, Wife

The morning of April 1, 1997, dawned bright and clear. Just as we were about to go out to milk the cows, the electricity went off. We shared a generator with our daughter Romaine and Vernon Oberholtzer. We told them to use it first as the milkman comes there first and also the silo crew was coming there.

Earl went over to Vernons and worked at chipping silo staves till Vernon was finished milking with the generator. The electric came back on just as they finished so Earl came home. He and I did the milking together like usual—only later. Milking time was often a time of visiting and sharing thoughts. In the last several months Earl had often mentioned that if he ever had serious head injuries, he would rather die than linger on. Two of our relatives were having struggles after having had head injuries.

Son Earl Lamar and daughter Lucille finished their chores and ate breakfast awhile. Lucille went off to school and Earl Lamar went to help with the silo building. So Earl and I had breakfast alone, our last meal together. He said he will be so glad when this silo is finished. It seemed to be heavy on his mind. After breakfast he rested a little, while I hurried with the dishes. He then went over to the silo-building. I went to daughter Lois as she had a doctor appointment for two-week-old Carol. She was born prematurely and only weighed four pounds and eleven ounces, but was doing fine. I had offered to take them to the doctor as her husband was busy.

While we were sitting in the doctor's waiting room, the phone rang. It was Lois' husband with a message for us that there had been an accident. Earl had been hit on the head by a falling silo stave. He said, "Earl's still breathing but it doesn't look good." They had called the ambulance. I was to leave Lois at the doctor's office where her husband would pick her up. I was told to go right to the hospital. So I hurriedly drove those 20 miles.

All that went through my mind over and over again was, "Lord, that Thy perfect will would be done!" When I got to the hospital, they were working on Earl. I was told that the helicopter was on the way to take him to a larger hospital.

Our whole family then started on the two-hour drive to that hospital. As we gathered there in the hospital waiting room, we learned the details of the accident.

The work on the silo had reached a height of 50 feet. On the ground Dad, Nevin, and Vernon had finished stacking staves on one side. Dad had sat on a pallet to rest. At 52 years, he remarked that after this, silo building was for the younger generation.

Up on the silo, the men set another row of staves in line and busied themselves getting the hoop in place. As it was being assembled one end came loose. It swung around the silo knocking three staves loose. At the same time Dad got to his feet, picked up a stave and carried it to the stack that was already finished—we shall never know why. There was a shout from the top, but not enough time for Dad to move, or even look up. One stave struck him on the back of his head as he was partially bent over. The men were at his side in an instant. It seemed that life had already fled. But then he gasped and began breathing again. The neighboring minister came over, and as they waited for the ambulance to arrive those present gathered in a circle around Dad while the minister led in prayer.

Finally, after several weary, anxious hours of waiting, the doctor came to talk to us. Our faintest hopes fled as he kindly explained our dear husband and Dad's condition to us. He told us they were doing all they could to keep his blood pressure higher than his brain pressure. Earl's brain was swelling and already extensively damaged. They could do surgery to remove his skull bone and maybe avoid more damage, but even then his chances of survival were very slim and he could never lead a normal life again. Of course we said, "No," to the operation idea. We knew Dad would never want that. They had no indication that his brain was functioning at all, and his condition was getting worse. We could only pray for strength and courage to face the hours ahead, for we knew parting with our dear one would come.

Then two or three of us were allowed to go in and see Earl at a time. Gazing upon the still form, with tubes and wires everywhere just didn't look right. His arms looked strong and brown—his face tanned—yet, there he lay, already in the stillness of death. Thankfully we could not see much of the injury as it was on the back of his head.

"My dear, faithful husband! Must I part with you?"

In the night that followed we tried to rest or sleep here and there on the floor and chairs of the waiting room. The night was a long and weary one. Finally daylight came. The nurse told us the pressure in the brain should not go above 20, but by morning Dad's was 130. There was no way his brain could be alive. We requested that the respirator be removed and were told we would need to wait till the doctor came out of surgery.

How thankful we were for the support of the ministry and family who came to spend those waiting hours with us! Also we were so thankful for the many prayers that were ascending on our behalf. We could not have handled it without them.

In the afternoon they finally told us they would be turning the respirator gradually lower. About 5:30 p.m. they took the respirator off and everything stopped. Those words, "It's all over," sounded so final. Fresh tears were shed as we faced the truth. Our dear husband and Dad was gone. Yet as we gazed upon his dear face, still and silent in death, we knew God makes no mistakes. Before starting the two-and-one-half hour drive home, we all gathered in a circle in the waiting room while our minister led in prayer. We were reminded, "His grace is sufficient!" Those words would encourage us time and again in the difficult months ahead.

Earl's funeral was April 7. As we gathered around that still form one last time, we wept—not as those who have no hope, no for he had left a good testimony and an example for us to follow. We wept because we would see his face no more.

Yet as we considered the accident, over and over we could say: "If only he hadn't walked over there at that moment—if only he had been one step one way or the other—if only that stave hadn't fallen at all..." But the timing was not man's timing, it was not man's mistake, and so we can only think, "Behold, the hand of God!"

Oh, the comfort that is felt as friends and relatives come from near and far to share our sorrow. Sorrow was not new to our family. Just three-and-one-half years ago, a dear son, John David, also answered the call of God at age 24. He had battled with cancer one-and-one-half years. He was married and had two small sons. Now six weeks after Earl's funeral, John David's widow, Erla remarried to John Abram Martin. Their wedding day held such a mixture of emotions, (joy and sorrow). We were happy for Erla, and the boys would have a daddy again. Yet our grief was still so fresh in our hearts. These little grandsons had loved to go with Grandpa to the sale barn or elsewhere. He had tried to do what he could to help our widowed daughter-in-law. He, with the help of family and friends, did the work of building a house on the property Erla had bought. Then when she remarried they moved to a farm. So the house was rented out. Two years later, my youngest son got married and took over farming the home farm. So Lucille and I are now living in that house. Lucille is now 15 years old. It is truly marvelous how the Lord does provide. While my dear husband was still here, he was unknowingly building this house for me.

We still miss our dear loved ones very much. But with taking one day at a time and trusting in the Lord and submitting to His will, life is continuing on. We again can smile and enjoy the grandchildren.

"The eternal God is thy refuge and underneath are the everlasting arms" (Deuteronomy 33:27).

—*Mary H. Martin*
Memphis, Missouri

IVAN W. MARTIN
March 30, 1961 to November 30, 1998 (37 years)

Our Red Sea
Rebecca Martin, Wife

Monday, November 30, 1998, dawned like any ordinary day for a happy, healthy family. We had no way of knowing what a sad and tragic ending this day would bring. That forenoon our maid, Miriam, was doing the laundry. I passed through the washhouse with a load of wood and paused at "the gift of love" as Ivan had put it when he so happily brought in some grow light shelves which he had made for me in the last two weeks. My thoughts were, "What if Ivan should die before they are completely finished? Could I bring myself to get someone else to finish them? Or could I bring myself to use them?" But immediately another thought followed, "Yes, I'd ask brother Isaac to finish them exactly as Ivan had planned to make it. And I would want to use them and always lovingly cherish them as a true 'gift of love'."

Then I went into the kitchen to prepare the noon meal. As I was peeling potatoes by the counter, I couldn't shake the feelings of death and parting. If there was a parting to make, I hoped Ivan could go first. I would have pitied him to stay if I would go first. These death thoughts were not anxious, but they were peaceful and passing, and I let them lie as I so often had before. I finished making the noon meal, already expecting Ivan home any minute with a smile and a "Hi." But dinner was eaten without Ivan, because he had a chiropractor appointment and was not back yet. After dinner I started getting worried. So I went over to the "doddy" house to my single sister-in-law Valina. We looked down the road, but could see no bike. At least I felt better to know someone else was also worrying. I was coming back into our kitchen when I saw a policeman coming up the sidewalk—right away I knew! I mechanically went to the door. "Are you Mrs. Ivan Martin?" "Was Ivan riding a bike?" "Yes." Knots and lumps were filling my stomach and my mouth went dry. My heart cried out, "Please, just hurry up and tell me if he's still living!" The policeman went on to say that Ivan was hit by a car and had very serious head injuries. They were planning to airlift him to a larger hospital. The police offered to take me to the hospital. I needed to identify him. Numbly, Valina and I got ready to go. I was breathing wordless prayers. How good it felt to have Valina along, although she had to leave in the midst of making gingerbread boys for a bakery order. Wayne (4) awoke from his nap. He seemed to sense I was unable to baby him for he didn't fuss to see me go away. On going out the door I wanted to say some parting words to Miriam (maid), but none came. None were needed. Our feelings had no words; we all felt the same.

The police wondered if there is no one I want to let know before he takes me to the hospital, so we first went up the road one-half mile to the shop to tell my father. At least now someone could pray for me. Dad would have liked to go with me but his clothes were dirty and I felt I was not alone with Ivan's sister Valina with me.

On the way to the hospital all I could think of was, "How serious is this going to be? Will there be a long recovery, or will the Lord take him home? Oh, please save him. You know, God, how much I need him and love him. You know what a happy family we are."

We whisked past the traffic as they responded to our flashers and pulled onto the shoulder. I noticed the policemen were changing the traffic light to green so we never wasted any time.

Arriving in the emergency room, the police led the way to Ivan's side. He was lying on the stretcher with an oxygen mask to help him with his breathing. They told me his heart and lungs were in good shape, and my hope rose. As soon as I had identified him, Ivan was whisked away from us to be taken to the larger hospital by air. Valina and I were taken to another room where there were questions to answer and papers to sign. I could think of nothing but to be at Ivan's side again as soon as possible, but the policeman recommended that I go home to family and friends to make further plans. Ivan would be in surgery a few hours anyway. So the policeman took us home again with much less speed. But before we came to the lane we saw my father's "dachwagle" (top buggy) going out the town line toward home. We caught up with him to tell of our plans and wondered if my brother, Isaac, could go along to the next hospital. I felt scared going to such a big, strange place without Ivan with me. Then we asked the police to drop us off at the shop, because we needed to do some phoning for a driver and also to ask Mrs. Nelson (Ivan's sister) to come stay with Ivan's mother for the night. His mother's mind was completely gone and she was helpless from strokes.

Then Valina and I walked home together, shivering, wondering, praying. A bakery customer came driving by and stopped, hoping to give us a ride. I thought, "Oh no, I need a little time for myself before I go home." So Valina went with her to tell her what had happened. The customer and her husband had lost their son, (same age as Ivan), only three months before.

Neighbor Mrs. Clayton went to school to let our children know about the accident. The two teachers took our three children outside to break the news, then they were allowed to go home so I could talk with them before I started off for Hamilton. Would I be gone for days? I packed a bag and hoped I'd need it. Soon the children came home full of worry and questions. This was the first time I felt like crying, but for the sake of the children, I tried to be brave. The first question was, "Is it worse than Luke Metzgar's bike accident?" Of course I didn't know. "Do you think he will die?"

Death was not new to the children. Ivan's brother Peter died one year before, so they knew that God takes Daddies home to Him. I told them I do not know if he will die, but they are not to worry too much. "Try to be good boys and girls until I come back again."

Driver Enos Brubacher came to get me. My sister-in-law, Saloma, came to stay with Mommy (Grandmother). I felt relieved to have a "mom" here with the hired help and the children. Another neighbor, Preacher Paul came to go to the hospital with Isaac, Valina, and me.

Now the long ride began and reality struck me. Oh, how I wanted to think Ivan would recover, but deep in my heart I knew he would surely die. I started praying, "Not my will, but Your will be done, for Your name's sake I will suffer. Give me grace to stand this test." Memory after memory came flashing through my mind. Only yesterday Ivan had made one side of the Weber family scrap sheet which was waiting to be done. Sometime earlier I had mentioned his sheet and wondered if he would like to start on it, but he said he would do it later, "It's almost too nice to sit indoors." Instead he wanted to play Andy, Andy Over with the children. So we all had a happy game of this and that. Soon our "Sunday with Mommy was spent."

Another Sunday afternoon came and I hesitatingly asked him again if maybe today would be a good day to do his sheet. (Our four children were riding a pony.) Immediately a smile flashed across his face, "Yes, that's exactly what I want to do!" This was only yesterday.

I'll always treasure our last peaceful, happy afternoon talking and humming, whistling, and munching on popcorn. He told me to search for some verses while he was gluing the picture of his choice on the scrapbook page. I could not find a verse with which he was completely satisfied, so I gave him the book and said it might be best that he finds his choice. It wasn't long until he had found four verses. "Now to print it on with my clumsy fingers..."

The one side of the page was now finished and we just chatted a while yet before Ivan went to the barn to get an early start on the chores. We knew we would have lots of "youngie" for supper because singing was at our neighbor's house. After Ivan was outside, I picked up his sheet and admired his work, thinking to myself, "If he would die now, he would have left a remembrance for the scrapbook."

Ivan was in a valley of sorrow over losing his dad, Ammon G. Martin, and four months later, a close brother, Peter W. Martin. He was struggling with grief and mentioning he had a great longing to talk with Peter once again. It was now a little over a year since he had so suddenly left.

Ivan asked me one evening if he would die as suddenly as Peter, if I think he'd be good enough to be called "a child of God?" I didn't doubt that he would, because he wanted nothing more than to live a Godly life. I told him so and he looked happy. A pang shot through my heart, "But you're not leaving me, are you?" But I didn't voice my thoughts. As long as your partner is living, you don't want to talk death. I thought, "Surely my thoughts of death are only because we had two deaths in the family in the last year."

One evening when Ivan was feeling sad, I sensed his longing for his departed brother. So I asked him what his prayer was. He answered, "I was thanking God that He has brought me into this dark valley so that I could stop and look over my past life and realize life is too short to be wasted."

Another evening after my chores were finished and before I went into the house, Ivan asked me to go through the barn with him. And there we went over our stock of animals together. He was showing and telling me of this and that about chores. When this happened two more times, "I wondered, Oh God, what does this mean? You know I'm not a barn girl at heart. Surely you're not making a widow of me?"

One Saturday evening when he came in after chores, he wondered if we wanted to take a family walk out the bush lane. We had been taking these strolls now and then while the children were studying the stars at school. But since the children were only starting bathing yet, I told him we'd better go along another evening. So he said he would just go alone. He started leaving, then said "Bye, see ya'." Then he paused at the door and added, "Hopefully." Then he was gone. I could not forget that look on his face, neither the last word he said. But I reassured myself that surely nothing could happen to him on the bush lane. He came back from his stroll and I forgot all about it until now, on my way to the big hospital. "What does all this mean? Why are these thoughts coming back to me?"

The automatic doors closed behind us. We were shown the way to a large waiting room with lots of people and a large television blaring. After half-an-hour of waiting, wondering, and praying, a doctor came to the door and took us out in the hallway where I noticed, not one doctor, but a team of doctors! We were ushered into a "quiet room." My heart was pounding wildly, fearing the worst. Why does it take a team to say he is doing well after a successful surgery? Already I thought I knew the outcome.

The doctor kindly informed us what he had tried to do, but things were not turning out well. It would likely be only a matter of hours anymore. Ivan was losing out fast as he was being transported to the larger hospital. So as soon as they had him in their hands, they started life-support. Before the doctor left us alone in the room, he mentioned organ donation. "Oh no," my heart rang out. I was hoping for good news. Now I had to think of this already! "How can I, when up until now I had always thought organ donation was such a scary thing to consider? Oh, how can I wisely make such an important decision?" I breathed a little prayer, wondering what Ivan would say to this. I got the answer! I knew he would help anybody wherever and however he could. It was not hard anymore to say, "Yes, I consider. You may use what you can. Maybe someone else can live through his death." Then I felt at peace.

The first time we went into the ICU to see him, it didn't look as if there was much life left. But the nurse at his side told us how he's in such good hands. "Oh please be honest. We know he can't get better. Please Lord, take Ivan home soon. Don't prolong this. Please take him!"

The night wore on, but time had no meaning. How good it felt to have brother Isaac and Preacher Paul with us. Oh, how I dreaded to have Ivan linger for days, and have Isaac and Paul leave us alone. Although when I voiced my thoughts, we were assured they wouldn't leave us. Again we trudged down the halls to Ivan's room with heavy hearts. This time they were losing his body warmth and were using heat blankets. His face looked so battered and his head so swollen. He felt cool to my touch. "Oh, dear Ivan. Are you really leaving me?" Oh, how I would have liked to go with him! But I knew my four children, ages four to thirteen, needed me.

Around 11:00 p.m. two doctors came to the quiet room to tell us that Ivan is now brain dead. Oh, what a relief of joy and sorrow. The woman doctor looked very unfeeling, as if it were a daily chore, but I knew she couldn't handle life if she were to put herself in our shoes each time things like this happen.

For the third and last time our feet took us mechanically along those halls. Ivan's chest was still rising and falling as he needed to stay on life-support until they had the organs they needed. But his body was already growing cold. Oh, what a jumble and tumble of thoughts. Can this really be true, or was it only a bad dream? How could I go home and face a funeral and life without my husband? If ever I needed him, it was now!

Again we waited in the quiet room. After some time a woman came with papers for us to sign for organ donation. She was very kind and praised us for not being too selfish to consider this important step, but I cringed at the word "harvest."

Back home again at 2:00 a.m., reality washed over me full force. I was back alone—no husband to lean on. Mrs. Nelson, Miriam, Valina, and I sat together in Doddy's kitchen so as not to awaken the sleeping children. We shared and wept until four o'clock in the morning. Valina told how I shared with her a few times that I wonder what God is preparing me for. (I did not remember this anymore.) The others were ready for two hours of rest, but I could not go alone, so Miriam went with me.

The road sign at the orchard was constantly waving and clanging in the strong wind. The night was over with, although I had not slept. Angus, the hired man, came down the stairs first while I was combing my hair. I had to break the news to him. He was shocked as he hadn't realized the seriousness of it.

I felt a strong urge to spend some time with the children alone before other people started coming. But, oh, how my heart ached and bled for their awakening. I went upstairs with a heavy heart. First I went to the girls as they were not sleeping soundly. As soon as Erma (13) saw me, she knew. I did not have to tell her. We wept together. Then Laurene (8) said so bravely, "But I'm still glad Luke Metzgar didn't die because Lydia (his wife) doesn't have children." Luke had also had a very serious bike accident one month previously. The children didn't know Lukes.

Just the day before Ivan died, Erma said that when she and Dad drove the pony together before school, he had told her, "Keep on driving Dusty every morning, but I will not drive Dusty anymore. He listens better when you drive." Dusty was a new pony which the two of them were breaking in. She also said a few nights before she dreamed that Father had died. And the last while she had felt so sad all the time. Even her school friends were no longer a comfort to her.

I went over to the boys' room. Again we wept together with not many words from Laverne (10). My heart broke for him, losing such a kind and loving daddy. Wayne (4) was so full of questions which I answered for both Laverne and Wayne. One question was whether Daddy went to heaven in a helicopter. (They knew Daddy had been taken to a Hamilton, Ontario hospital via air transport.) I helped the boys get dressed and come down to the kitchen where I weakly tried to prepare a breakfast, for which no one was hungry. Already I put one plate too many on the table as I set it.

My parents, Ishmael Webers came early. Oh, how I pity them! This couldn't be easy for them. I hoped mother's heart condition could take this.

People started coming to prepare for the funeral. My thoughts were far from all the work which had to be done. How good it felt to leave it all to others.

Both sides of the family began to arrive. Only a year ago we were in those shoes when Ivan's brother Peter died of a heart attack. I know so well how they felt to come to a house of mourning. I would have liked to shield them all from this pain. Even so it felt good, very supportive, to have them surround me.

My only sister's words were comforting, expressing how Ivan had "prepared" for this. Of course, my sister-in-law, Mrs. Peter Martin held a special place in my heart, since we were cousins and friends from childhood and had ended up marrying brothers. Peter and Ivan had farmed side-by-side for six years before Peter and his wife moved onto their own farm in Mount Forest. Now they have both left, leaving each of us with a family and a farm and many memories. It felt so good to have her sit beside me. She knew the painful sting of death and also the peace which God sends.

That afternoon Mark, the driver whose vehicle hit Ivan on his bike, and his parents and stepfather came. Oh, how my heart went out to this 19-year-old lad. Such a load for his young shoulders to carry! "Oh God, please carry him through this so he can forgive himself." I could plainly see it was God's will. Mark said he doesn't usually go home for lunch, neither does he drive that route to school. His parents didn't know he was coming home for lunch.

The first person to come upon the scene was a stranger to us. She came to the viewing and funeral. She told us she had had a dream. She heard someone say, "Ivan died." She phoned to the Ivan of their family in the morning to see if her dream had been telling her something. He told her he was fine, but she still couldn't shake off her dream until she found out that this stranger was named Ivan.

The next morning the coffin came. Wayne, at four-years-old was very excited and could hardly wait to see Ivan. I was surprised that I could see very few bruises. Peace flooded over me. No matter how hard it was to go on without him, I could not wish him out of his peace. Truly, our loss was his gain.

At noon when three rows of nephews stood behind each other around the coffin for five minutes, I couldn't help but to think what Ivan would likely have said, "Come, learn something from this."

It was a long day—no sense of time as friends from far and near came and went. My body was tired and drained from stress and weeping and loss of sleep. Evening came and I fell on my knees to pray a wordless prayer, as there were no words to match my feelings. But God promised to see my distress and He felt my need. He understood my wordless prayer.

The next morning, December 3, 1998, loomed large as dawn broke a little dreary. The weather matched our moods, but it was still mild for that time of year. All week the temperature stayed between 50° and 70° F's with no snow or mud, and people could be outside.

I had wondered who they would ask to drive our carriage to church on the funeral day. This choice looked very big and real to me. Who could take Ivan's spot on this day? When I was told my brother Elo Weber would take the team and carriage, I had mixed feelings. The big release brought tears, but my heart went out to him. Their life is surely not an easy life either. His wife, Edna so often did not feel well enough to go along due to her brain tumors. Truly God's ways are not our ways.

At church, people, and more people paid their last respects. And now the time had come for us—one last, final look. I had been dreading this so much. It hardly seemed fair that at such a sacred time in life there was so little privacy. But when I stood up from the bench that my family and parents were sitting on, I strongly felt God's presence. Peace and strength washed over me. Oh, it felt so heavenly! The walk to the grave seemed like walking through the Red Sea. There was no way out, or back—no other way, but through the path that my Lord will make. I found I had strength to take the children to the edge of the grave to show them how shallow the grave really was. Four-year-old Wayne always thought the grave was very deep and there was a river at the bottom which "rushes" the body away, away. Now he saw the wooden box and whispered, "I'm glad Daddy's coffin will not get dirty."

The sermon felt like ointment on my bleeding, torn heart. My tears were all dried up.

The next day it was so nice and warm that Laverne and Wayne were sawing and pounding away on the ramp. Around noon they came in to show me their work. A complete birdhouse made without a pattern or help, and nearly perfect. They wanted to make a gift for Mom—following Dad's footsteps.

Mommy Weber, my mother, shared how on Sunday night she awoke from hearing someone knocking three times. Although she knew the knock wasn't at the door, she went to look and saw no one. In the morning she had forgotten all about it, but when she learned of the accident Monday it all came back clearly.

This experience has brought a lot of tears, but I want to take God's ways as they come and hope to meet Ivan again.

—*Rebecca Martin*
Waterloo, Ontario, Canada

Oh, grant me faith, dear God of grace
that strengthens and sustains.
A faith that reigns triumphantly through
all my earthly pains.
Grant comfort that reveals Thy love
Console my heart I pray.
God, wipe my tears and courage give
to walk in hope each day.
Oh, grant me peace, dear God of grace,
peace, Thou alone cans't give.
That I may rest my soul in Thee
and in Thy sweetness live.
Amen

-Selected

"The Lord preserveth the strangers; he relieveth the father-
less and widow: but the way of the wicked he turneth upside
down (Psalm 146:9).

LAVERNE BRUBACHER
April 10, 1957 to February 10, 1983 (25 years)

Have Thine Own Way Lord
Mary Brubacher, Wife

The day dawned bright and clear, crisp and cold. A fresh new day—a gift from God—Thursday, February 10, 1983. Little did I realize the deep sorrow that would press upon my heart by nightfall.

Laverne went out into our little barn to feed the sows and piggies while I packed his lunch and prepared breakfast. Our breakfast was sprinkled with casual conversation. In exactly two months, April tenth, would be Laverne's twenty-sixth birthday. The following day, April eleventh, Carl would turn one year-old. The two most dear and near people in my life could celebrate birthdays so close together! However, foremost on my mind was which household task I should pursue today, the laundry or the weekly baking? These were my Thursday and Friday jobs. With such bright sunshine the diapers which I used for our precious ten-month-old Carl, would dry nicely outside. Yet it would be so cold to hang them out. Perhaps tomorrow the temperature would warm up a bit, so we decided I would bake instead.

We were discussing such trifling matters when our time together was running short, but why not? *"For ye know neither the day nor the hour wherein the Son of Man cometh"* (Matthew 24:13b).

Pausing in our morning routine for our good-bys, Laverne picked up his lunch pail and headed off to work. He drove truck for a local feed mill where he worked for six years. He was an ambitious yet cautious driver. At this point he drove the tanker truck which gave him shorter runs closer to home and more regular hours.

The first I knew, Laverne was back—standing in the kitchen doorway. "Remember, I'm coming home early. We want to go out to Elmira to the Blood Donor Clinic. You won't have to prepare supper tonight as we will go down to my parents." He lingered, standing there with his broad smile.

"Yes, I'll try to have Carl and myself all set to go."

"I'm coming home early!" Oh, for Carl, for me, for family, for friends, etc., "It was much too early Lord! But for you, Lord, it was right on time! Laverne didn't need to donate some of his blood! You wanted his soul—today!"

I decided I would bake some apple pies and bread. How Laverne loved homemade bread! In my mind I already anticipated the pleased look on his face when he tasted his first slice. With these happy thoughts, deep peace enfolded me. Later, looking back, it was an unusually deep peace—a calm before the rough water.

Then came the phone call. I detected a heaviness in my mother's voice as she casually started the conversation. "Cheer up!" I thought. "It is such a beautiful sunny day!"

The message? "It appears Laverne is trapped in a steel grain bin full of corn kernels on Lorne and Ralf Shantz' farm near Baden. But they are not sure until they find him. They will cut a hole in the bottom of the bin and empty it. You will get another phone call soon."

Laverne had the tanker truck running and was inside the bin with the hose, sucking corn kernels out of the bin into the truck. Lorne, a familiar customer, had crawled up the outside ladder of the 20-foot bin to visit with Laverne, then left for fifteen minutes. Upon returning, Lorne couldn't find Laverne inside the bin, nor anywhere else. Meanwhile, the hose wasn't drawing corn anymore. In this short time span the unexpected happened. Laverne had suffocated in the corn kernels.

Many thoughts raced through my mind. My mind was like a yo-yo preparing for the worst then back again to—perhaps an injured husband. I numbly remember Carl sitting in his high chair, while I fed him his dinner.

The next phone call came with the heart-rending news of Laverne's death.

My parents came as soon as possible. Laverne's parents, more family, and ministry followed. Friends stopped in. How could I pick out songs to be sung at my dear husband's funeral? It could not be! One, of the two which was chosen, was, "I Need Thee Precious Jesus." Oh, how well the poet expressed my thoughts.

The "clock of life" had seemed to stop as I laid my beloved husband in the cold grave. But in reality it ticked on. Life seemed so short since the time we so joyously pledged our marriage vows exactly one year and seven months before on July 8, 1981. Laverne was so fond of his little son and helped care for him. Such precious memories ended so soon.

Family and friends from far and near shared and helped carry the burden of sorrow in so many helpful ways. I felt unworthy of all the kindnesses shown. I could never repay it all. Truly I could say with Job of old: *"The Lord gave, and the Lord hath taken away; blessed be the name of the Lord"* (Job1:21b).

Yet at times the months and weeks ahead loomed like mountains. How could I go on with what seemed as one-half of a person, and with only one-half of a heart? But wait, I only needed to take one day at a time or if that was too much, one hour at a time, or just one minute at a time. The Lord would provide sufficient strength.

The first year without Laverne seemed exceptionally long. But time and God are great healers if we are willing. Over the years I could more fully understand Psalm 30:5b: *"Weeping may endure for a night, but joy cometh in the morning."*

For a long time I put off baking bread. When I thought back to that morning, I was kneading the bread dough, punching it this way and that way to knock out the air bubbles; little did I realize the Lord wanted to "knead" my life to fit a different pattern—to shape "my loaf" according to His choosing. I now again enjoy yeast baking. It always fascinates me to watch the magic of yeast. The lump of dough is so ugly and sticky. Mix the proper ingredients, add the yeast, let the dough rise, and the end result: a beautifully formed, round loaf of bread. So may Christ be the "yeast" in your life and mine. May the Lord add the "proper ingredients" and just the right amount of blessings and trials so that we may "rise" (or walk) in the path according to His will.

—*Mary Brubacher*
Wallenstein, Ontario, Canada

DAVID SHANTZ
November 23, 1951 to October 27, 1992 (40 years)

His Appointment
Valina Shantz (Wife)

"When thou passest through the waters I will be with thee and through the rivers, they shall not overflow thee; when thou walkest through the fire thou shalt not be burned" (Isaiah 43:2).

As the summer months of 1992 faded and October drew nearer, my mind kept pondering memories of October 1982. The circumstances where I found myself were similar to those of my sister Leah's only ten years before. After seven and one-half short years of marriage, her husband Angus Martin died in a farm accident leaving her with three small children. I keenly felt our family of three now had the same ages: Calvin (6), Eugene (4), and Wilfred (18 months). David and I would be married for seven and one-half years. Again, an ordination was coming up. Even the sun set with the same vivid hues in the autumn skies. A certain feeling of apprehension settled over me.

The last few winters, David was battling throat infections. Checking in about allergies had been discussed several times, but the doctors didn't seem ready to go on with that route yet. That fall his throat was causing problems earlier than usual. He was on penicillin again when our family doctor said, "We can't go on like this. There is a limit to how much a person can take!"

An appointment was made to see a specialist. After a number of tests were performed, the specialist commented on David's otherwise good health. They scheduled him to have his tonsils removed sometime in December. The doctor reassured us there should be no cause for alarm. Later, due to a cancellation, the surgery date was changed to November 23, 1992 (David's birthday). When David learned about this he said, "It's not a day too soon!" But the Lord had another appointment.

David was also in the hospital on his twenty-first birthday resulting from a farm accident claiming his right arm. With time his elbow, back, and knees seemed abused from lopsided working. I often wondered, "What will the future hold? Would we have to sell the farm?" David's one-armed ways were unique. He had a prosthesis which I later discovered I really missed. At a young age our boys learned they had to back up to Dad to be held. They also knew they had to hang on if he scooped them up, and hang on they did! Often I'd watch them head for the barn, David and his three sons. Would things hold together until the boys were older? I tried to tell myself that the boys' boundless energy would be a big help someday. It had always been David's dream to have a farm, and thankfully his wish was fulfilled.

The Orvie Shantz (David's family) gathering was planned for August 29, 1992, at David's sister's Elo and Edna Weber. Because of weather conditions and late harvesting that summer, a debate arose about postponing, or canceling the gathering. David hoped they wouldn't change the day. The day is a precious one in my memory. During the forenoon singing, David again chose the song, "Does Jesus Care." How it tugged at my heart! There already were links missing from this family circle. A seventeen-year-old brother, Harvey, died of encephalitis at the time when David was baptized. Orvie, (David's dad) a wheelchair patient for thirteen years, died just a little before we started dating. Brother Maurice died of a heart attack at age 40, two weeks after our wedding day. Several years later his wife died of cancer leaving two dear nephews and a niece without parents.

One Sunday evening we did our chores early and went to sister Leah's for supper and chores. This visit always brought back memories of the years I had stayed with her and her children before our own marriage. As we left her place that evening David said, "We must do this more often." On the way home, talk centered around our concern for Leah with small children to raise and a dairy farm to operate. David felt this was really too much responsibility for a woman, but we could never come up with a better plan. It was not new to hear him talk like this.

In September Calvin eagerly started to school. Soon the first parent-teacher meeting came up. To my disappointment, a salesman showed up and I went to school without David. My thoughts turned to Leah, knowing she had gone alone many times. Later, as David quietly slipped into the classroom amidst the other men, it struck me full force how very pale he looked in comparison to the others. Was this yet another incident to help prepare me for what lay ahead?

Corn-cutting time came. David did not feel up to helping the neighbors harvest our own corn. Another round of throat infection brought the second kind of penicillin. Filling the bunk silo left him very tired. This was strange, as previously he could easily put in long days. I always helped put down the plastic, but this time I also dug the trench around the outside and carried straw bales to seal it off. I gladly did this for David, but it was not typical of him to let me do the heavier work. Then he decided we would do the chores yet before supper, as he was ready for bed early that night. The feeling of foreboding gripped me.

On Monday, October 19, David wanted to get ready for garden plowing, even though he hardly felt well enough to do it. He had asked brother-in-law Elo if he could do our field-plowing. David was concerned that he would not get another infection before surgery. I helped clean out the horses' pen to cover strawberry rows and perennials, etc., for winter. I found this time of working together special, but it left me with the same sinking feeling. Could this be the last time we would do this together? Did the boys, too, sense that their time with Dad is running out? It seemed Calvin and Eugene couldn't be with him enough. Even Wilfred had changed from a "Mama baby" to a "Daddy's boy."

David had another doctor appointment on Wednesday, October 21, and came home with more penicillin. He was told to take it easy, so I did more of the barn chores. With the throat infections, he also had sinus problems. This time he got a very upset stomach.

Friday, the twenty-third, he was back to the doctor and was given medicine to help settle and soothe his stomach. He had also started with a deep cough that didn't let him lie down that night. He tried hard to spit up phlegm into the sample bottles the doctor gave for testing, but it proved almost futile. So he moved to the recliner for the rest of the night.

Saturday forenoon, October 24, was the last time David went to the barn. He showed me different things so I could continue with the chores. Then he broke out in a cold sweat, which left him very weak. He sat on a hay bale for a while, but we decided he had best head for the recliner again. Elo came to inject cattle which we had just bought.

Saturday evening the doctor told David to discontinue penicillin, and gave him a strong cough syrup instead. Tylenol was recommended for fever. He tried drinking garden tea, ginger ale, or chicken soup base drink, but nothing wanted to stay down. His body was growing weaker. He requested a mustard plaster for his chest. Sometimes we used fried onions and the hot water bottle, too, so it would heat even more. That night he phoned his mother. She also must have let my parents know, as later they wondered if they should come here for Sunday instead of going to church. We didn't think that was necessary, and wanted them to continue with their previous plans. I brought a foam sheet down to make an elevated bed on the living room couch, for lying down made David's coughing worse. I was reluctant to leave David, but he encouraged me to go upstairs to sleep in our bedroom so I'd be closer to the boys. How he also must have prayed during these restless times...

Sunday morning, the twenty-fifth, he was booked for chest x-rays. After x-rays a suspected stomach tumor was ruled out, but a slight case of pneumonia and chest infection was detected. I wondered if he would be able to come home again. But this was not our family doctor. (I think he would have moved him on by now.)

Back home again, the hours together were so sacred and precious. I can't describe the feeling of this veil God had draped over and around us, concealing the future.

David could rest somewhat Sunday p.m. The boys did well to play quietly while I entertained them. They sensed that Dad did not feel well. Taking the boys out with me, we did the chores early. When we came in, I put the boys to bed. That night it was even harder to go upstairs and leave David. Silent moments of reverence were shared, which gave me much food for thought as I headed upstairs to bed.

His strong arm and hand hung so limp and sweating spells sometimes left a strange odor. "Oh, God! You know it all. I want to put my whole trust in You."

Early Monday morning, October 26, I arose and combed myself, apprehending a day with much in store. I mentioned the difficult night he had and wished I could have done more to make him comfortable. David answered with a faint smile, "It could be much worse." He did not have pain. Uncomplainingly, he bore this so courageously for the children's sake and mine, but most of all he remembered our Dear Saviour, a Shelter in the time of Storm! Words cannot describe the peaceful calm amid this "unknown." God's strength was felt so keenly, for his love is unfathomable beyond compare!

After I came in from the barn, David phoned the hospital from his recliner to tell how his weekend had gone. They told him that when the doctor comes on duty they'll give him the reports to see what he decides.

Then while we were trying to eat breakfast, David vomited blood. He phoned the hospital again and we had orders to come to the emergency room as soon as possible. He also phoned for a driver.

As Calvin was leaving for school, I followed him out onto the porch, not knowing when the next opportunity would be to converse with him. I tried consoling him with the thought that God was with us, while my mother-heart cried in silence. How could he concentrate at school with such a turmoil in his home life?

David's sister Mary, Mrs. Irvin Weber, phoned, so I asked if it's okay if Eugene and Wilfred would stay with them. In a daze I tried to get the boys' clothes together and to prepare myself to leave, too.

After vomiting blood David's mind was in and out. I helped him dress, for he had not realized that our driver was waiting for us. That was uncharacteristic of him. With all my being I hoped we'd get to the hospital soon and that he would not collapse on us. While going through the door I remember wondering if other people will be going through our house before I had a chance to be back home again. Traveling downhill, our driver was braking for the narrow bridge, when a car behind us, going at dramatic speed, rear-ended us. (Several years later that driver's husband was killed on the road.) We bumped and swerved around on the road before we finally came to rest in the ditch on the other side of Irvin's lane. Stunned, we crawled out of the van, thankful that we could still walk. The seats were all broken off and the driver's seat hit Eugene's head. I took the children in to Irvin's. From there we phoned our driver's husband. He and his son Peter came with the pickup truck. David had remained sitting in the van, but then he got out and up through the ditch alone. He had watched in the rearview mirror and knew better than we what had happened, but we could not wait for the police. Peter stayed with his mother while his dad took us to our small town's hospital. David walked into the emergency room, and he wanted me to go with him. That was the last he was on his feet.

We were sorry our doctor was not on call. Immediate action took place, with lots of blood samples, questions, solemn faces, and hushed talking. The situation was serious. They admitted David thinking his condition was stabilized, but you didn't have to be a doctor to see he was continuously getting worse. Several times I begged at the nurses' station for ginger ale for David's high fever and dry throat. His breathing was labored. They were waiting to do more blood work. They even brought dinner. With my help he forced himself to sip soup. Soon a cleaning lady, or whoever, came in and she noticed our dire predicament. The doctor was ushered from the emergency room. A portable x-ray machine was ordered into the room. Even oxygen didn't help his breathing much, and I was asked to leave the room. The dramatic change in the new x-rays from those of previous days was worse than the doctor had ever seen, so he phoned a larger hospital. David was moved to isolation, as they were puzzled!

They planned to move David to London, where the larger hospital could better care for him. I went to phone Mary. The wait till the ambulance came seemed like hours. I hoped I could go with the ambulance and not need to find another driver. The ambulance driver gave his permission, "If you can take it up front." Little did I realize that God would see fit to have another very close call only a few hours after our last accident.

I watched as my dear companion was wheeled out on the stretcher. A little over a year ago we had seen Eugene travel this way. Eugene was in the hospital for one month, a mystery then, but now we learned it was from strep throat infection that invaded his body. How well and good that the Lord sends life only a day at a time.

The miles to London seemed endless and the unknown so vast. I closed my eyes and tried to rest. "Be still and know that I am God." "Have thine own way, Lord, have thine own way." "Oft' the way to the goal seems so weary and long." These thoughts ebbed through my mind of turmoil, yet despite all this, wonderful strength and peace prevailed. As the ambulance sped down the highway, it was humbling to see the respect shown us as other vehicles moved to the shoulder of the road (all except the huge, clumsy-looking truck in front of us which was heedless of our siren or flashing lights) We veered around it once we could see that oncoming traffic had pulled onto the shoulder, only to have this truck merge over into our lane. A crash seemed inevitable! We must have scraped the mirror! The ambulance driver was quiet for a while, then he softly whispered a prayer of his own. Had the truck driver been sleeping? Probably we'll never know, but we were spared. I thought this is probably what an ambulance driver encounters every day but later while visiting with our head nurse, she mentioned she had never seen the driver so shook up before. (The head nurse and the doctor had gone along in the ambulance.)

Now we were pulling up to the hospital in London where the staff was prepared to receive David. Was he still conscious? With the hustle and bustle of attendants, I wondered if I'd be able to get a glimpse of him. From a distance I saw his face, and our eyes met... As long as life and a sound mind are granted to me, the memory of the serenity shown there, will not fade. It was our good-by without words! (I never could have said good-by to the one I loved so well.)

Then I was called up to the desk and stationed in another little nook to answer a fleet of questions. Later our nurse stated that without today's techniques in an ambulance, David would not have survived the trip. He was aware of their conversations but did not participate. The doctor was in the emergency room till they moved David to Intensive Care. Before leaving he came over to me presenting the verdict, "It's leukemia." Even though I was bracing myself, the verdict was a severe blow, as if someone had hit me in the chest. That ache was to stay for a long time. A continuing prayer was uttered heavenward. The ambulance was heading back to our hometown leaving us here. Is this how it felt to receive such a message?

Sometime later an assistant lady took me to the next floor. She suggested I should get a sandwich to eat. In the cafeteria they were putting up Halloween decorations. "How vain," I thought, "What different worlds we live in."

Then the lady showed me to the little "Quiet Room" off the hallway from the large waiting room. What a relief to get away from the turmoil of strange people! In the "Quiet Room" we phoned Irvin and Mary. Sister Leah was planning to come down with our driver.

In the meantime the doctors informed me of David's grim state. His chance of surviving was only 5 percent. He asked if I cared to see him. Of course I did, but it was with such mixed feeling. They were telling me the strongest dose of morphine allowable had been administered. David's body was purposely paralyzed to ensure immobility while the doctors worked on him. They kindly tried to prepare me, as I washed my hands and donned a garment. I was reminded to consider my words well, since an unresponsive person may still be able to comprehend! What a maze I was led through! Many beds were pushed in at any angle, all with severe cases, and holding somebody's loved ones. At the very back in the far right corner there was a hissing and purring of machines with tubes and more tubes! There was David with his head tilted back in such an uncomfortable looking position. A shunt was put in through his neck. Blood was oozing from his mouth and nose. Nurses stood with their hands under the covers for the few moments I could be in. "Is this my bosom companion?" I could not even get close to the bed. The words I had planned to say, did not come. "Oh Lord, if it is Thy will, release him from this agony. But if it is Your will that he lives, may I find help to accept seeing a loved one suffer." The many miles from home and the children left in the care of others seemed to loom high in front of me. Back in the "Quiet Room" the doctor asked about near kin. Finding a match for a bone marrow transplant would be easier since David came from a large family. Chemotherapy should definitely be started, only David's body was too unstable. Upon inquiring of his occupation they were not surprised to hear that he was a farmer. "He must've been a strong, healthy man, a fighter, or he wouldn't be with us anymore," asserted the doctor.

Sister Leah entered our small room with her driver. They had let Irvin and Leah's family know that David's sickness was Acute Myelogenous Leukemia. They did emergency leukophoresis, which is a screening of red and white blood cells.

Leah mentioned the stark sunset she viewed on the way and shared her feelings. Many times I had been comforted by pondering her experiences when she was poisoned eleven years before, lying very ill in this same intensive care unit. Leah also mentioned that my younger sister Elsie, Mrs. James Martin, fetched Eugene and Wilfred. Calvin stayed at Irvin's to go to school from there.

The doctor wanted my consent for a needle surgery, for despite all else they were doing, David's body seemed to be losing out rapidly. My permission was also given, when yet another "higher educated" specialist was called to the scene. He wanted to try a newer procedure which required three-fourths of an hour to do. They would rotate David from his back to his stomach, in hopes of assisting blood flow to necessary areas. The specialist said he'd seen bad cases before, but nothing compared to this.

Before the rotation began, Leah and I were allowed to see David again. Then I noticed a commotion in that corner. We were greeted with, "Sorry," and asked to leave. "We have lost his heartbeat!" I couldn't help but wonder, "Is David experiencing some heavenly rapture now? Would they revive him again or was the Good Lord calling him home?"

Out in the hallway a nurse asked us if we were aware how serious his condition was, because we appeared so calm. (How could we be otherwise?) "You must have a strong faith." Leah's circumstances were introduced. We said we were thankful for our heritage, and the Lord was our Strength! Definitely so, for He carried me on "feather pillows" all the way!

They were still busily occupied with David so we were shown back to the "Quiet Room." A nurse warmed blankets and brought us tea. A minister was introduced. How soothing he was to a tired, muddled mind! That little room seemed like such a hallowed spot! Has the Lord not promised that where two or three are gathered in His Name, there would He be in the midst of them?

Upon the minister's departure, Leah and I made beds on the floor and lay down. Although stiff and sore from whiplash earlier that day, I dozed off for a few precious winks. The familiar knock on the door brought me back to reality. Three doctors came in and their face betrayed their message.

"We are sorry, Mrs. Shantz. We tried everything we could, but your husband has passed away." Even now I can hear the doctor's foreign accent ringing in my ears. We didn't doubt they did all in their power and thanked them for their efforts. Again they marveled at the strength of the Lord! "You'd be surprised what all we meet up with when we bring loved ones such awful news," one of the doctors quoted, "—swearing, anger, bitterness, whatever."

Praise the Good Lord, I felt unworthy to have my prayers answered. David's pain-wracked body would heave no more. He was forever free from pain and care. There was almost a tinge of jealousy on my part, for now I found myself where I never wanted to be—a widow with small children! Now I had to go on without David, but God knew it all, and I still had Him! Oh, to go on though, with a painful, bleeding, severed heart. How could I function normally with half a heart?

Numbly we got our belongings together. The last chapter of our lives together had been lived and the lid of the book was closed. This was a new book!

We decided to phone for a taxi from Mount Forest as I was keen to get home before morning, if possible, and we'd be more comfortable riding with someone familiar, who knew the way. It was 12:40 a.m. Tuesday, October 27, 1992 when David's appointment was met, roughly eight hours after I knew of his diagnosis. Acute Myelogenous Leukemia starts in with severe sore throat, but since we had dealt with that before, the doctors had not been alarmed at first.

The nurse said that after they have David cleaned up we could go see him. So while waiting out the hours it took for the taxi to drive down, we had precious moments at the side of our loved one's form—so still. The radiance on his shining, smiling face, gives me courage many times to keep looking up and plodding on. How dearly I treasure this time in my heart. (It didn't compare with the viewing in the coffin after man had tampered...) David still felt warm and looked so natural, just as if a touch could awaken him, but alas, he had gone to join the heavenly throng! Oh, what a deep yearning of heavenly homesickness surged through me and I longed to join him. But there were three small precious souls at home. I could hardly wait to be with them again, but oh, the overwhelming responsibility... Somehow I would make it, but my heart ached to realize that once again children would have to go through life without their earthly father. I thought my heart was wrenched many times over Leah's experience. I found out the wrenching could get a lot worse—such a raw grief. It was my turn in the valley of sorrow, but Jesus was there. He was so real and so near. But Satan detested this close walk with God and was and still is ever so ready to stumble such a weak vessel.

A gentleman came in wondering if they could please do an autopsy because David's was such a strange case. I was thankful David and I had talked about this once. After reading an article, I had told David it makes me shudder. Surely we wouldn't let anyone do an autopsy. He said that, yes, he would if it could at all help someone else later on. So my consent was given and the papers were signed. I didn't have to decide about donating organs because disease had raged his entire body. They were now ready to move David on so Leah and I went down to the main front waiting room to wait out our time. Everything looked so bleak and quiet that night.

We were thankful to see our driver pull up. The Good Lord provided anesthetic to endure. We got home around 5:00 a.m. Yes, home, but was this the same home? I was in such a different world, a world with dulled feelings, and yet they were so sharp that it hurt to be alive. I wanted to live for the children's sake though and also for the Lord's. Twice my life could have easily been snuffed out that day! Time and earthly things meant nothing! Leah started making phone calls. Calvin heard the ring at Irvins' and came downstairs. Irvin brought Calvin home so I could break the sad story to him. What a comfort to know David's departure was God sent, it was not our choice to separate and see the dear boys suffer so! It was no wonder they had had so many questions of death, dying, and the hereafter. God was also preparing them for what lay ahead. Now I did not have to start at the beginning.

I got David's "things" cleared away. People started coming. Dear Grandma Shantz, David's mother knew what

I was facing. My parents were parting with another son-in-law. (A little before I turned four, our oldest sister died at eleven years old.) Brothers, sisters, neighbors, friends (ones we needed before) were also needed now. How unbearable if they would forsake one at such a crisis in life! Yes, it was a warm feeling of sharing, caring and working together. But a "bereft home" is such an upheaval for the family in grief, especially for small children. When moving out furniture, the boys wondered if they're taking all that away yet too? I yearned for quietness. My mind felt as if it would explode. Oh, to get away from this publicity!

I was thankful that with other people's help we could stay on the farm and the boys could be with me. Truly our God is the widow's God. He loves and He cares! How good it is that we do not have to understand His purposes but only need to trust Him.

It was touching, yet very thought provoking, when before the funeral I went to get "the will." I was baffled because I could not find that envelope where I knew it should be! Later I found it in the top desk drawer right at the very front. We hadn't had the opportunity to discuss things in David's last days. So it was comforting to read "the will" because it answered some questions that somehow had a way of surfacing. I wondered if David knew how ill he was. Knowing him, I felt he did. Then too, I felt David must have moved "the will" to the other drawer, which was as if he were reassuring me "all is well, I knew." *"For now we see through a glass darkly; but then face to face; for I know in part; but then shall I know even as also I am known"* (I Corinthians 13:12).

There have been many blessings through this experience. New friendships were formed and older ones were strengthened. The bond of our widowed sister's circle is very strong and inspiring. This experience completely took away the fear of death. Death, actually, in itself is beautiful.

On April 21, 1999, we parted with my father after a heart-related condition, then other complications had set in. So now Mother has joined her daughters in widowhood.

A deep sorrow can bring a great joy—a closeness to Christ that you don't expect and can't understand, much less describe.

—*Valina Shantz*
Mount Forest, Ontario, Canada

When God Calls A Loved One Home

The Lord has given, the Lord has taken,
Blessed be His Holy Name.
God has reached down to touch us,
We will never be the same.
When God calls and a loved one answers,
It draws our hearts together,
They leave all earthly cares behind.
To dwell with God forever.

The evening sun set on heavy hearts,
Time ticked on through the night.
In the early hours of morning,
Another soul took flight.
In our hearts we are thankful,
God saw that it was best.
No more trials, no more suffering,
But eternally—sweet rest.

Precious memories have been left us,
  His warm smile, his caring ways.
We will miss him, deeply miss him,
  There is an empty place.
Oh dear sister, our hearts ache for you,
  And your three small precious sons.
Oh Heavenly Father, help us to say
  Not my will but Thine be done.

God's ways are so much higher than ours,
  We do not always understand.
But the paths where He leads us,
  Are controlled by His Own Hand.
God has promised He will never leave us,
  Though trials thickly 'round us lie.
He understands our deepest heartaches,
  He hears the faintest sigh.

Ten long years, yet oh how short,
  It almost seems, time stands still.
So many things have been repeated,
  But we trust it is God's will.
Two widowed sisters, now amidst us,
  How heavy seems their load of care!
Through the days that lie before us,
  Oh comfort—sweet hour of prayer.

When God calls a loved one Home,
  The parting causes tears to flow.
We could not wish them to return,
  When they have seen heaven's glow.
Thus our longings grow much deeper,
  To join those gone on before.
Heaven's glory shines ever brighter,
  Oh to meet—and part no more!

-Elsie Martin

PAUL S. HOOVER
October 10, 1934 to May 1, 1981 (46 years)

God's Leading
Ruth N. Hoover, Wife

Trust in the Lord with all thine heart; and lean not unto thine own understanding. In all thy ways acknowledge Him, and He shall direct thy paths. (Proverbs 3:5,6)

The year of 1981 brought many changes in my life. I often think, "We do not know what is in the future, but we do know Who holds the future."

Living on a farm is a busy life, and we enjoy it, but things can change so quickly. It was springtime and Paul was thinking of soon planting corn, etc. In the meantime he was working on the farm truck, making sure it would be in good condition for farm use. I noticed he was getting big black and blue spots several places over his body, but they weren't sore, so maybe they soon would disappear.

One week later on a Monday morning he seemed rather tired and said his urine was very dark colored. I called the doctor right away for an appointment, thinking it might be a kidney infection. When he came home from the doctor that afternoon, I took him right to the hospital. There they admitted him and did some tests.

Wednesday they transferred him to a large medical center. There he was diagnosed as having leukemia. Thursday they did a bone marrow test and prescribed chemotherapy. We, as a family, were all in to see him that evening. It was the last time we could talk to him.

The next morning I got a call from the hospital saying that Paul had gone into a coma. By the time our children and I got to the hospital they had him on life-support. I stayed at the hospital all that day and night.

Friday morning the doctor came to tell me Paul had passed away. He never needed to take chemotherapy treatments. He went to be with the Lord. In a week's time he was gone.

"Must I go through this experience again?" Exactly ten weeks before our son Stanley had been killed in an automobile accident. It was on a Friday evening and he was on his way home from Numidia Bible School. And now this. "Why?" I just wanted to question the Lord, "Why this?"

I knew I had to be courageous for the sake of my children, but oh, the grief and sorrow I had to bear. It was also hard for them. They, too, were hurting so much from losing a brother, and now they had to part with their father.

We got many letters and words of encouragement and many deeds of kindness were shown from our church family, brothers and sisters, and others. Just knowing they cared meant so much.

Eighteen years have now passed. My son is doing the farming. Three of my daughters are married and the youngest is teaching school. I also have grandchildren to love and enjoy.

A verse that means so much to me is: *"As thy day so shall thy strength be"* (Deuteronomy 33:25b). It is a reminder to take one day at a time. May we all be ready and looking for our Lord's return.

—*Ruth N. Hoover*
Myerstown, Pennsylvania

We Can Say God Led
(In memory of Paul Hoover)

We can say,
  God knows just what he's doing
  When He sends a child so small,
  That is filled with words of cooing,
  That is joy and fun for all.

We can say,
  God knows just what He's doing
  When He gives him strength and mind,
  That makes a man of intellect,
  And yet so meek and very kind.

We can say,
  God knows just what He's doing
  When He joins two different souls,
  In marriage and in harmony,
  With deepening love, as years do roll.

We can say,
  God knows just what He's doing
  When the sun sends joyful rays,
  And our life is what we wanted,
  And our wish, becomes our ways.

But, can we say,
  God knows just what He's doing
  When He takes before our eyes
  That dear soul, the one we love,
  To His abode, in yonder skies?

Yes, we can say,
>*God knows just what He's doing*
>*When our plans are crushed and dead.*
>*He will lead tho hopes are shattered,*
>*And will give us grace instead.*

Yes, we can say,
>*God knows just what He's doing,*
>*Not because we have our way.*
>*But we know that God is leading*
>*For our best; We'll take His way.*

-Myron Martin

(The death of Myron Martin is recorded on page 247.)

"God is our refuge and strength, a very present help in trouble" (Psalm 46:1).

EARL M. MARTIN
April 22, 1968 to March 3, 1998 (29 years)

Where Your Treasure Is, There Is Your Heart Also
Nancy Martin, Wife

"Be still, and know that I am God." I was reminded time and again, of these words after my husband's accident. Nothing happens that is not His will.

Our family numbered six: Earl and I and our four boys, Edgar (4), Abner (3), Orvie (2), and Aden (six months). We were trying our best to enjoy these little boys given into our care while they were small. At times it did get a little trying to always have the correct amount of patience and wisdom.

We lived on a farm consisting of 80 acres and we rented 30 acres. We milked an average of 25 cows. Because Earl's work did not keep him busy at home, he would go on construction jobs with his dad's crew.

We had heard about a few accidents the winter before his death. I can clearly see and hear him say, "Dad's crew has been really lucky. Very few people have hurt themselves. But someday it will also happen in our crew." I remember thinking, "Yes, I believe so, but who will it be? It can't be my husband, and besides we already have three young widows in our community. We couldn't have another. These things always happen to other people, not to us."

Spring construction work began March 2, 1998. They wanted to work for Earl's Uncle Aden Martin to raise an old barn and replace the foundation. I knew, and Earl knew, it was a risky job but he was ready to get back to work. It was not my policy to say when he may go and when he may not.

So we got up early and knelt for prayer. I especially prayed for Earl's safety that morning, then we quickly went about our morning duties. Having him ready to go out the door at eight o'clock sometimes kept us hopping. During the day I sometimes thought of him and hoped all would go well.

The Co-op phoned that day to say they want to bring seed grain the next day. I said, "Oh, that's okay. Earl will be at home tomorrow." He had a dentist appointment at 11:00.

At 5:30 that evening the call came from the boys and also myself, "Daddy's home!" Everyone ran to the door or windows trying to get attention first. I needed to wait for my turn although we had eye contact when he did come in.

When he heard about the seed grain, he phoned The Co-op and said he wants to go to work but he will make room in the drive-shed and they can just put it there. He really didn't need to be here. He told me to cancel the dentist appointment.

That evening at the supper table Earl was telling me how this old barn creaks and groans when the frame is being lifted. He said, "It is a little scary." To myself, I thought, "It's not in vain that I pray a little prayer for his safety." He said, "Tomorrow is another dangerous day, then the worst is over."

The next morning, March 3, we got up early again, stopped for prayer and to myself I thought, "It went well yesterday, it will go well again," never realizing...

We did the milking together as usual. It was not unusual for Earl to ask me, "What are you going to work today?" This morning he did too. I said, "I'd like to cover those books with plastic for the children. Quite soon it will be spring and I didn't get that done this winter." The smile he gave me is one I'll never forget. I like to think it's with that smile that he will greet me in heaven.

We hurried about our morning work. Only the baby was awake yet when we ate breakfast. I felt a closeness, just the two of us, usually we would be kept busy helping the children. Edgar got up yet and helped a bit to get the drive shed ready for the seed grain.

I can clearly see Earl walking through the barnyard, down the road and out of my life. I always had in mind that I want to see him leave so that if he wouldn't come home again I'd have that memory. This morning was no exception. Sometimes everyone would want to say good-by and he would say good-by to everyone till I sometimes wondered, but this morning I can't recall any good-bys. Thus, I continued my morning duties.

I was working at my books around 11:00 when suddenly I remembered Earl's dentist appointment, so I called and canceled it and scheduled it for the following Tuesday. It was almost 11:30 when I heard footsteps on the porch. I was in the other end of the kitchen and as a rule I always look out the window into the barnyard whenever I walk through the kitchen. I didn't this time which was probably good, or I would never have made it to the door. I swung the door wide open and saw Earl's parents, our minister, and the police cruiser in the barnyard, all at one glance. Immediately my heart screamed, "NO!"

My mother-in-law took me in her arms and said, "Oh, Nancy, Earl's gone. The barn collapsed." I quickly ran to collect the children who had gathered in the bedroom where the baby was waking from his nap. Then we sank into a rocking chair. My parents also soon arrived with a taxi.

The men left again for the scene, as Earl was still underneath at the time. We ate a little lunch and after dinner neighbors and friends started arriving, and then slowly reality started to sink in. Only then did I cry. The news was broken gently to me that we might not be able to have a viewing. Oh, I wanted to see his face one more time, but not if he didn't look like my Earl.

It was planned the funeral would be Saturday as we had four other funerals in our church that week, all older people.

Thursday morning we went to the funeral parlor. There our two fathers decided we'd leave the coffin closed but we could touch his hands. I held Earl's hand. It was stiff and cold—no return clasp. Again reality struck.

At 11:30 the coffin was brought to our home. As it was brought in the door, I thought, "This is not the way we usually greet Daddy. No shouts of, 'Daddy's home!'"

The next few days were filled with meeting people. Friends and family were a wonderful support and I appreciated all the people that took time and effort to come our way. But, oh, the longing to have things slow down and return to our regular life, but that was never to return.

Saturday morning dawned unusually warm for the month of March. "Today is the day my husband will be buried. Yes, my husband!" I felt discouragement almost taking over. We did not yet have a death in either of our families. It had always been other people who had to give up. I had often wondered how long my family of fourteen and his family of six would stay complete.

A short service was held in our home in the morning and then we went to our church for burial and services. Many words of comfort and encouragement were shared. I could well feel, "Where one hurts, we all hurt." Oh what would we do if we wouldn't have a church and Jesus Christ to lean on!

The next day was Sunday. We went to church, although it would have felt good to stay home and rest but I also felt it wouldn't be easier to face people if I'd wait longer. It was very soul-enriching to be there. For dinner we went to my sister's place. She is married to Earl's brother. In the afternoon the family all went to the accident scene. Again reality struck! Yes, there lay the barn in a heap. We could well see the accident was out of man's power when we saw where all the other six men were, also underneath but none of them seriously hurt. Yes, God still performs miracles.

I thank God that family and friends have provided so that we can remain living on the farm where all our memories of working together remain. God has carried me through many a dark valley and the way seems too long and hard. Many times I need to remember to take my burden to the Lord and leave it there.

A few months later while I was struggling with loneliness, we had our annual school picnic. The whole school section would come together for an afternoon of softball and afterwards ice cream. I managed to put up a good front during the afternoon, but in the evening when the children were all in bed and the house was quiet, the flood gates again opened and I wept uncontrolled. When it seemed my heart would break, a robin started singing cheerily outside the window, "Cheer-up, cheer-up!" I felt like throwing something at that bird. "How can you, and how dare you sing like that?!" But then I remembered who sent that robin and who made him sing. I thank God I did not stay bitter for long. Thus, I was once more comforted.

Many times God carries me through when the way seems too dark and He will continue if only I can put my trust completely in Him. Where He leads, I'll follow. Many people say, "Take only a day at a time," and I thank God that's all that's needed!

I want to willingly carry my cross and labor for Jesus till we too shall be called to rest.

—*Nancy Martin*
Mount Forest, Ontario, Canada

Must Jesus bear the cross alone
And all the world go free?
No, there's a cross for everyone,
And there's a cross for me.

-G. N. Allen

"He is despised and rejected of men; a man of sorrows, and acquainted with grief: and we hid as it were our faces from him; he was despised, and we esteemed him not. Surely he hath borne our griefs, and carried our sorrows: yet we did esteem him stricken, smitten of God, and afflicted (Isaiah 53:3-4).

Another Account Of The Death Of Earl Martin
Ervin B. Martin, Father

Tragedy struck our family so suddenly on March 3, 1998 claiming the life of our oldest son. It was a cool, damp morning when our driver picked us up to take us to my brother Aden's farm. We had started jacking up his barn the day before so that a new wall could be put underneath it. Our daughter Eileen also went along to our second oldest son James' house which was on the way. With us were Lloyd, Allen, and nephew Paul. Next we went to pick up Earl. He was walking down the road to meet us, as he often did, rather than waiting for us.

I remember thinking, "His steps seem slower this morning. Is something wrong?" He climbed onto the back of the pickup with the boys. After we dropped Eileen off at James', Earl sat in the front of the truck with the driver and I for the remaining three miles. Earl sat beside me, as he had many times before, but this time I had a feeling I cannot explain. Only God knew what the day would bring.

We started our work with more jacking of the barn. My brother Aden and two sons plus a neighbor man were also helping. In our way of thinking everything was going well, although jacking old barns was a job I have never really liked. We stopped at approximately ten o'clock and discussed how much higher we wanted to go. We decided to jack another four inches, then be satisfied.

How well I remember! Earl and I were on the back side of the barn and he asked me if he should jack there. I said he could come to the front and help me. We jacked there, working together. We had just finished setting a safety post in place, and were planning where to set up next when it happened.

We were about eight feet inside on the south end of the barn. Earl was six feet behind me. I was looking up and all of a sudden saw movement in the top of the barn. I dashed out the doorway. By the time I was outside, the complete barn had collapsed with one loud crash. In all my years of taking down barns, and sometimes pulling out the frames, never had any gone so fast and so suddenly.

An indescribable feeling came over me. There were seven men under that collapsed barn!

After what seemed a while, though it was only a few minutes, the first men came crawling out from under the debris at the side of the barn. Soon everyone was out except Earl and Jonas. Jonas called and said he is okay. I called Earl's name a few times, but got no answer. Oh, again, a feeling I can't explain... Jonas could see Earl and said, "It doesn't look good."

How can I describe the next little space in time as we became sharply aware that Earl had been so suddenly called away? Life was gone. Oh, the reality!

When we became aware that life was gone, my first words to the others were, "Gott macht kay mistakes." ("God makes no mistakes.") Little did I realize how hard I would be tested with that statement. As I think back, I know that God was surely right there or we could not have remained sane. I think we experienced just a little feeling of what our Saviour experienced in the Garden of Gethsemane: "My God, my God, why hast thou forsaken me?" The helplessness of knowing my son was trapped under the barn and not being able to do anything about it, even though we knew he was not suffering. Death had been instant.

A feed salesman was there to talk with Aden and dialed 911 on his car phone. Oh, the pain I was feeling as we waited for the police, firemen, and ambulance, but I knew there was nothing they could do.

Finally, a police cruiser came, and then another one, also firemen and ambulance. Allen had a little bump on his head, so the ambulance took him to the hospital for observation. No one else had as much as a scratch. It was not until later that we thought to say, "What a miracle that no one else was hurt."

By now Lloyd and I decided that I should go and tell Mother and Oscar, who were at home. A policeman offered to take me. It was both a long and a short ride home. How could I tell Mother? It surely was only through God's help that I was able to go on. After meeting Mother and Oscar at home, we went to Melvin Bearinger's next door. He was also our minister. Mother, Melvin, and I went with the officer to tell Nancy, Earl's wife. Oh, the helpless feeling and pain as Nancy and Mother met. I can't explain it. My prayer is that God may supply what is needed for anyone that comes to such a time in life.

About ten minutes after we arrived at Nancy's, her parents came by taxi and had our daughter Eileen along. Each meeting of a family member brought uncontrollable tears. To meet in such a way...

The police officer then took Urias Weber and me back to the collapsed barn where Earl was still trapped underneath. Oh, if I could just take him in my arms again as I did when he was a little boy! Lloyd came to me and said that the policemen and firemen are not letting anyone close to the barn. They thought a high-hoe was needed to move part of the barn in order to remove the body. Pat, an officer whom I had become acquainted with, came and asked if we were sure we want to stay as it would be a while before the body could be removed.

Oh, the pain in my heart! Even though I knew Earl was not in pain because body and soul had parted, I could not bear to leave the scene now.

I asked Pat for permission to let us remove the body. After consulting with his sergeant, they decided to let us go ahead. As we started to move debris, one of the firemen came forward and said they have air bags to lift the beam. So with their help the removal was made. I was very grateful for their help. The undertaker was also there to take away Earl's body.

We went back to Nancy and her four little boys. How could things go on? By now neighbors and friends had gathered to make plans for a funeral. What would we do without neighbors and brothers and sisters of the church?

Mother stayed with Nancy the first night. As I lay in bed alone, sleep would not come. The pain in my chest was so unexplainable, a physical-mental pain. "My God, my God, why hast thou forsaken me?"

Thoughts of Earl came to my mind, how he had grown up as our son. We had trials and many joys also. He grew up into manhood, was baptized and received into church membership. Then one Saturday evening he told me, "My life is going to change. I will be taking a girl home on Sunday evening." We were very thankful about his choice, and I wished them God's blessings. It also gave us as parents another responsibility. The time came when Earl told us that they would like to be married and start their own home.

Many thoughts came to me as I lay there in bed. From Earl's boyhood days he was always ready to go, wanting something to do. He was not particularly the leader, yet he was always ready to do his part. Perhaps he was not a leader then, but was he not a leader now? As I thought back to the collapsed barn, my thoughts were, "I'm sure he looked back to see how the other boys were faring as the barn was going down. He was a man concerned about his brothers and other workers. I thought of him as a captain that goes down with the ship. Yes, surely he was our leader." With these thoughts I drifted off to sleep.

I received a call from a widow in our community before I had gone to bed . She wanted to share a thought with us. This widow told me what another young widow had experienced when her husband had been suddenly killed in a car accident, and that there was no viewing. (We already knew there would be no viewing because of Earl's head injuries.) That widow had been allowed to touch her husband's hands. She always wished that she had given her little son that experience as he later asked, "Was Daddy really in that black box?" So she thought she would like to let us know of that experience. I was very grateful that she brought this to our attention.

We talked about this the next day at Nancy's before we went to the funeral home. Should the two oldest boys go along? Edgar was almost five and Abner was three. What impression would it make on them? Nancy said she would ask them and let them decide. Yes, they wanted to touch Dad's hands. This would be their only opportunity because after we as a family had been to the funeral home, the coffin would be brought to the home and would never again be opened.

Yes, it was a time I surely would not want to have missed. We went to the funeral home with our family, James and Selema, Lloyd and Irene, Nancy, Edgar, Abner, Oscar, Allen, and Eileen, plus Nancy's father and mother. There I again related to them the thoughts that came to me last night, how Earl was our leader and we trust we could some day all be gathered together in that heavenly home.

Earl's body was brought to the family home on Thursday at noon for visitation in the afternoon and all day Friday.

As I think back now, oh, how thankful I am for a caring and sharing community, neighbors, and church brothers and sisters. People from different walks of life came, too.

Saturday, the day of the funeral, was another nice, calm day. There was a short service at the home conducted by Melvin Bearinger. Then we had services and burial at Cedarview, our home church. The ministry who had part in the services were from our home church, Michigan, and Pennsylvania. We very much appreciated all those present from far and near.

Life is going on although it will never be the same. We thank God for His many blessings and the strength He has supplied to continue on. May God be praised!

—Ervin B. Martin
Mount Forest, Ontario, Canada

"But though he cause grief, yet will he have compassion according to the multitude of his mercies. For he doth not afflict willingly nor grieve the children of men. (Lamentations 3:32-33)

PETER MARTIN
August 29, 1957 to July 25, 1997 (39 years)

When God Calls A Loved One Home
Minerva W. Martin, Wife

I can still picture them clearly as they headed for the barn to do the evening chores: Peter (my husband) in the center, and Daniel (6) and Verna (4) on either side, their small hands clasped in his larger ones and skipping along beside. Soon, thinking the pace too slow they let loose and ran ahead.

I remember thinking Peter's limp, (the aftereffect of a broken heel six years earlier), is surely not getting better with each passing year. I wondered if something could be done that he need not feel so tired in the evening after a full day's work, or was it age creeping up on him. After all in another month he would have his 40th birthday.

Later I wondered if his tiredness came more from other things of which we weren't aware.

The next day, July 25, 1997, started in just as any other day. At dinnertime we talked of different things, about the funeral the day before for a 10-year-old girl that was run over by a tractor, and then we recalled different tragedies that had happened over the years. We also remembered that today four months ago, on March 25, Peter's father passed away quite unexpectedly from a stroke. This was our last meal together.

Later in the afternoon the hired maid we had fetched the week before, was out roto tilling the garden. Daniel and Verna were playing in the freshly turned soil. The other children were gone for the day.

Peter was working in the basement in a crawlspace under the kitchen, putting support to the outside wall. Later in the summer we wanted to add a small addition to the house. He came up several times to fetch something, and the last time it was for light bulbs. I told him, "I wish you had a nicer place to work." He answered, "It won't be very easy, but I'll start once and see how far I get." About 15 minutes later I was working in the kitchen mixing a cake and musing as I worked, thinking of the busy months ahead with house building besides another little one to care for.

My thoughts went to my husband working in the basement. I listened for some sound of him at work and heard nothing. Everything was silent, strangely silent. I quickly finished the cake and put it in the oven. I listened for some sound from the basement again, still nothing. I felt I must go and see what he's doing. I looked at the clock as I headed for the cellar door, the time was exactly 3:00. I felt an unusual peace and calm as I descended the steps and went to the place where he was working. I had a feeling all might not be well, but I didn't feel at all afraid. There he was, lying on his back in a very relaxed position, just as if he were resting. I asked if something was wrong, but I got no answer. I called his name several times and touched his face and shoulder, but there was no response at all. Fear gripped me, and I wondered if the death angel had touched down and claimed another soul. Already I felt at a loss at not being able to ask Peter what I should do next. An ambulance was called and Peter was rushed off to the hospital. I went along. My thoughts were busy, swinging one way then the other. Inwardly I knew he was gone, but then I'd think,

"No, he can't be. God knows how much I need my husband yet, I can't go on alone with a family and a farm." Then I thought of others in much the same circumstances who were widowed. "But they were more capable," I reasoned. "Surely this time they can revive him again."

At the hospital, they hustled Peter into the emergency room and sent me to the waiting room. I found myself sitting on the very same chair as Peter had been sitting on the day before, while I met my appointment.

The doctor soon came in and led me to a quiet room. There he started filling out a form. He said they did everything possible, with no flicker of response from Peter. He then went on to say, "I suppose you realize your husband has passed away." I heard myself saying, "Yes, I realize. And I'm sure you did everything in your power." At the same time I felt as though someone had pulled the plug and my whole being was drained. All hope was gone.

A nurse offered to call a family member. Soon Peter's two brothers and their wives came to the hospital. Together we went to see Peter. There lay the dearest on earth to me, cold and lifeless. The marriage bond we had made 15 years before was severed, and "till death do us part" was now reality. The man I had learned to love and appreciate, with his steady, easy-going nature had left me, and I entered this foreign field called widowhood.

The cause of Peter's death was not certain until the autopsy revealed that he had a bad heart, the result of a damaged heart muscle. He never complained of chest pains or not feeling well. As far as I knew, he was a strong healthy man.

Once at home, neighbors and family soon started to come. The children were brought home, and I went to meet them as they entered the kitchen with stifled sobs. I longed to comfort them, but words failed me. The boys soon left the house to look after the chores. One of them soon came in and whispered to me. "It seems Dad was preparing for this. The steer pen is cleaned out and nicely bedded, and the trough is filled with silage."

People were in and out all evening. Not much was said, only sympathizing silence. In the kitchen a few people were making funeral plans in hushed tones. An obituary was written for the next day's paper. My numbed mind wondered if this really was the same home that had seemed peaceful and sheltered just hours before. What an abrupt change!

Sleep did not come to me that night. My mind would never completely shut off. Many thoughts drifted through my mind. "What was Peter thinking when I saw him several times in the last weeks, leaning against the barn door after the evening chores were finished? Was he just relaxing and watching the sunset, or did he have deeper thoughts? Or what was he thinking when I had seen him standing, admiring a double rainbow?"

The next stressful days were a haze of activity and people, some preparing for the funeral, others sharing our grief. All was needful, for what would we do without community support? I still marvel at how much work was done, and I was rarely asked questions about preparations. How thankful I was that others went on and did the planning.

The children preferred being outdoors watching the activity of people coming and going—less emotional scenes.

Many people came to pay their last respects. Now and then a wave of reality would flow through my heart as a complete family lingered at the coffin, or when a father led his small child by the hand. Then I'd wonder, "Will I never again see Peter leading his small sons?" The future loomed dark and endless. "How will I ever manage alone?" Then the words would come that so many people whispered to me those days, "It's possible by taking one day at a time." Again I would feel such deep peace that it almost didn't seem right at such a time of turmoil. We owe God thanks. How gently reality sets in—bit by bit, just as we are able to handle it.

On August 1, four days after the funeral, Matthew, a chubby baby of 10 pounds, was born making a family of five boys and two girls, ages up to 14 years of age. He has been a cheering ray of sunshine and I felt the children's minds were kept occupied by his arrival. They have always enjoyed his baby ways.

Other activity also soon started as people encouraged me to go on with the house building. So with the help of many kind friends the project began and help kept coming till even the smallest jobs were completed. The compassion that was shown at that time, and since, has sometimes been over-whelming.

My oldest brother, Noah and his wife Lydia who have no family, unselfishly offered to move a trailer here and live with us till the boys are older. This offer was humbly, but gratefully, accepted, making much less responsibility for me.

In looking back now, one-and-one-half years later, I understand that grief has different stages and that time is healing. The constant heavy ache that I felt from the first thing in the morning till the last thing in the evening is gone. It didn't leave suddenly but gradually like the dawn after darkness. Now I feel more relaxed to come and go in my position without being constantly reminded of Peter's absence.

The first year held such mixed-up feelings, some things I would be dreading for a long time, like the first parent-teacher meeting, or a family reunion, or Christmas. Then when the time came it wasn't as bad as I had expected, but then the next time, reality hit hard at the most unexpected moments: the first time communion, or going to town alone, or discussing the next year's crop, or similar happenings.

There are still times, and I believe it will always be so, that certain things pain the heart. It is especially painful when someone else must walk the valley of sorrow.

My wounds seemed to be completely opened lately when Peter's younger brother Ivan (37) was taken out of time into eternity after a bicycle accident on November 30, 1998. After the funeral and at home again, I found the intense feelings wore off sooner. The void was not in our home. We did hurt deeply for the sorrowing mother and her four children. *"God is our refuge and strength a very present help in time of trouble"* (Psalm 46:1).

We will always have many precious memories of the two departed brothers and memories seem to grow more sweet with time.

A deep grief can actually be a blessed feeling when earthly matters become so small and unimportant and the Mighty work and ways of God so close and real. Then the heart is cleansed from all selfish evil thoughts and feelings. We would almost like to cling to that feeling forever, but poor mortals that we are, we could not stay in those realms forever and keep on living.

So long as life is granted, we want to willingly keep on with our earthly duties, and strive for that eternal reward, which is awaiting us.

"But though He cause grief, yet will He have compassion according to the multitude of His mercies. For He doth not afflict willingly, nor grieve the children of men" (Lamentations 3:32-33).

—*Minerva W. Martin*
Mount Forest, Ontario, Canada

When loved ones go ahead of us
It's hard to say good-bye
And in our grief and sorrow
We are tempted to say "Why"?

But they have found the peace and joy
This world can never give
And in God's heavenly home it's they,
Not we, who truly live.

-Author Unknown

"Trust in the Lord with all thine heart; and lean not unto thine own understanding. In all thy ways acknowledge him, and he shall direct thy paths (Proverbs 3:5-6).

EMMA MARTIN
March 1, 1962 to July 8, 1985 (23 years)

VIOLET MARTIN
January 21, 1979 to July 8, 1985 (6 years)

I Need Thee Precious Jesus
Orvie M. Martin, Husband & Uncle

Emma and I had been married for almost two years and Emma's sister Malinda had come for the summer holidays to help with gardening and to sell produce. Malinda was a school teacher and school was past toward the end of June so she came to spend the summer with us.

On Friday, July 5, 1985, we went to town and when we came home, Mrs. George (Almeda) Martin, Emma and Malinda's sister, was here and had their two youngest children along, Matthew (eight) and Violet (six) who wanted to stay with us for a week's holiday. Emma and Violet were close friends because Emma had worked at Georges' before we were married. When Almeda was ready to leave for home, Violet said good-by to her mom a couple of times as Emma stood holding Violet and watched Almeda disappear out the lane.

Monday, July 8, started in as usual and we went about our work. I remember hearing Emma and Malinda sing the song "When The Sun Sets Over Jordan" while they were working. It caught my attention because I didn't know the song. In the days and weeks that followed, the words of that song stood out with more meaning than when I had heard them singing it.

It had been a warm, humid day and in the evening Emma, Violet, and Malinda planned to go wading and splashing in the gravel pit which is next to our farm. Matthew and I planned to go for a swim at my parents' pond which is about two-and-one-half miles from here. I bridled the horse and as I was ready to back out of the stall, Emma came in front of the stall, reached between the bars, held out her hand and said, "Good-by!" This was not so strange that it startled me, yet it was unexpected just then, because I was leaving only for a short time in the neighborhood. She had a most precious, sweet, angel like smile, and with that we PARTED.

Matthew and I enjoyed a refreshing swim and as brother Joseph and I were talking, we heard an emergency siren roaring up the road, but we couldn't see what it was from where we were in the barnyard. After I had untied the horse to start for home, our neighbor's car came dashing in the lane and stopped beside us. Our neighbor lady jumped out and said, "Orvie, we have very bad news, your wife and niece are in the water and your sister-in-law came for help." She seemed urgent, so Matthew and I got into the car and went with her to the gravel pit. On our way I said to her, "Just remain calm, we are all in God's control."

I was startled as we came to the entrance of the pit and saw a scene of police cars, two ambulances, and fire trucks at the water's edge. I couldn't sum it all up because I didn't know of any water that was deeper than waist-deep, but this made me quite uneasy.

As I came to the scene, Emma and Violet's lifeless, pale bodies were on the shore and authorized men were trying to revive them. I soon found out that there was a seven-foot deep dugout test-hole where they got into. They were wading with all three side-by-side holding hands. Violet was in the middle. None of us knew about this dangerous hole. All three of them stepped down at the same time and had no footing. As they were struggling to get out, Malinda could feel Emma was also trying to help Violet get out, but they didn't have good footing and neither of them knew how to swim. Malinda thought she was going to drown because she had started to take in water already, but after a short time of desperation, she got a footing and got out, but she was unable to help the other two. The water was now still so Malinda ran across the field to the neighbors' for help. Emma and Violet had been in the water about twenty minutes until they were rescued.

Not long after I arrived at the pit, they loaded the bodies into the ambulances and headed for the hospital, then the fire chief took me to the hospital. As we were on our way, my mind was in a spin and pressure was increasing as reality was dawning, but I didn't want to let go as long as I didn't receive the final word.

At the hospital, a chaplain accompanied me into a private room and after a short time a doctor entered the room, though a stranger to me, he took my hand and said, "I'm Doctor ____, and I've very sad news for you." He paused, then said, "Your wife passed away. I'm very sorry for you. We did all we could." I asked, "How about the little girl?" He replied, "She, too, passed away."

Now truth struck in a lashing way, it seemed like I was up against a dark impassable wall with curtains pulled around and hardly any light. By calling on the Lord, it was bearable, for "underneath are His Everlasting arms" with love and compassion.

I was allowed to view the bodies and there on stretchers they lay. I immediately went to Emma's side and put my hand on her chest—no life, no breath. I put my hand on her forehead, no response. I went to her other side and took her right hand, but she did not return any feeling—cold, lifeless. This tore at my heart. Always up to now she responded in a happy, loving, way, but now she lay there lifeless and cold, never to return again, never to share again, never to love and be loved. It seemed so impossible! I turned my thoughts to the Lord and tried to plea for help. Although it helped to turn to God, it did not remove the dark shadow. I felt so alone in this strange place until my parents and Violet's parents came to the hospital where we then together shared our sorrow in sobs and tears. How our hearts were bleeding! After the first sorrowing tears were shed, we made an effort to return home, but it seemed that we were on an altogether new and different road of life on which we had to find our way in this strange and untrodden path.

As of yet I haven't found words to express the experience of coming home, to walk in the sidewalk and enter the house with my dear wife now having departed from us and departed from her mortal body into the Promised Land. It was with a very heavy heart, with a large hollow, a vacuum, and it almost seemed as if life and time would stop for us too. However, we were still here and had to go on. My parents had come along home with me for the remainder of the night, so we went to my bedside and knelt in prayer. We opened up our hearts to God and let our tears flow. I thanked God for many blessings that night, and I dearly thanked Him for granting me the opportunity to share life this short time with my dear wife, which He now had so suddenly plucked out of our 'midst. That night the Lord blessed us with the peace of acceptance and the peace of surrendering our will into the plan of God. However, life still looked almost impossible, but by giving our entire life and being into the Hands of the Lord, we trusted there would be a way for us who remain.

The poem, "The Red Sea Place In Your Life" was a help to me and it is still a precious pillar of trust to this day, but I've also failed in many ways, too.

It was an overwhelming experience to be able to sleep during these sudden adjustments, although the first night was next to sleepless. I felt it was none other than the many prayers of friends and the blessing of our loving Lord to grant us a deep sleep at night.

The few days before the funerals seemed to pass slowly and heavily and the tears came freely as the many friends cared and shared. In a way it wasn't so hard on the day of the funeral for the parting was already being made the days before. I seemed ready to have the body taken care of and words of consolation came from the sermon to soothe our weary minds and yearning souls. Emma's funeral was on Thursday, July 11, 1985, and Violet's was at Georges on Friday, July 12, 1985.

It was a comfort to us to know that Emma's thoughts were easily drawn to God, although she was an erring human who needed the grace of Jesus.

About six weeks before Emma's departure, on two different mornings about two weeks apart, we saw a beautiful bright rainbow in the western sky. The one end of the rainbow seemed to come down in our field, and the bright colors were on this side of the evergreen trees. As we stood there side-by-side admiring God's wonders, Emma was especially moved and enlightened with these symbols of God's promise and said she has a desire to go down into the field and stand in the rainbow since it looked so close and so pure. Emma had remained, admiring the rainbow even after I was continuing with the chores.

To accept and to surrender my will to the Lord had to be done again and again. The difficult and painful adjustments seemed to be harder and continue longer than it did to accept the accident as sent from the hand of the Lord. But in all these things I failed time and again, but God in His mercy and grace was always ready to forgive and help along again when I reached out my hand to Him.

It was a help to me to read of the struggles and adjustments that are common when in sorrow and grief. It helped to know that some struggles are a normal part of healing which is acceptable in Christian lives. But it is also necessary to be on guard to not let Satan snare us with "whys" and "self-pity." In the little booklet, "In Grief's Lone Hour" by: John M. Drexler, I found a lot of helpful information.

Never before in my life were my feet so unexpectedly wiped out from underneath me, and I never before experienced God's presence so real as when called to this lot in life. It is still a sacred and special place in my life to look back to, even though it cost a great sacrifice.

During these times my thoughts were often drawn heavenward with sacred meditations. It seemed like part of me went with Emma but I was unable to pass through the gateway to the future with her. Even though there was pain in parting from my beloved wife with many yearnings and lonesome times of giving up and adjusting, I honestly couldn't wish her back into this world.

"Thy Will Be Done."

—*Orvie M. Martin*
West Montrose, Ontario, Canada

Note from the author: Emma and I had no children. In June 1988, Esther Martin and I married. Our first baby was a stillborn daughter born in November 1989. (She was stillborn due to a blood disorder.) We have since been blessed with four sons and two daughters.

"Let not your heart be troubled: ye believe in God, believe also in me. In my Father's house are many mansions: if it ere not so, I would have told you. I go to prepare a place for you. And if I go and prepare a place for you, I will come again, and receive you unto myself; that where I am, there ye may be also. And whither I go ye know, and the way ye know. Thomas saith unto him, Lord, we know not whither thou goest; and how can we know the way? Jesus saith unto him, I am the way, the truth, and the life: no man cometh unto the Father, but by me." (John 14:1-6).

The Red Sea Place In Your Life

Have you come to the Red Sea place in your life,
    Where, in spite of all you can do,
There is no way out, there is no way back,
    There is no other way but—through?
Then wait on the Lord with a trust serene,
    Till the night of your fear is gone,
He will send the wind, He will heap the floods,
    He says to your soul, "Go on."

And His hand will lead you through—clear through—
    'Ere the watery walls roll down,
No foe can reach you, no wave can touch,
    No mightiest sea can drown;
The tossing billows may rear their crests,
    Their foam at your feet may break,
But over their bed you may walk dry shod,
    In a path that your Lord will make.

In the morning watch, 'neath the lifted cloud
    You shall see but the Lord alone,
Where He leads you on from the place by the sea
    To the land that you have not known;
And your fears shall pass as your foes have passed,
    You shall be no more afraid;
You shall sing His praise in a better place,
    A place that His hand has made.

-Author Unknown

MARTIN FOX
January 14, 1953 to September 26, 1993 (40 years)

Everything Will Be All Right
Ella M. Fox, Wife

Though I don't find it easy with my reserved nature, I will try to open myself up to write for the sake of others. I have really appreciated what others have written of their experiences. I wrote a short account of our experience over the time of my husband's funeral for my children's sake. Family and friends who went through losing a companion advised me to do it. I'm glad I did, as now, five years later; I have forgotten many of the details. So I'll try to take a little from what I had written.

Two years before Martin passed away, we moved to New York from a small 17-acre farm in Pennsylvania. We moved onto a farm consisting of 150 tillable acres and got it ready for dairy. With seven children to keep busy, we felt the farm was the best place to raise our family.

Toward the end of September 1993, about a week before his accident, Martin and I were doing the evening milking. Our oldest child, Miriam (16), was away all week helping to pick grapes. She usually helped milk in the evening. Now I took her place and enjoyed helping milk for a change and wondered why I didn't help more often. With the little ones it seemed to work better with Mother in the house, and the older children helping outside. Martin and

I enjoyed the time together alone those few evenings and discussed many things while he did the milking and I did the dipping. I can't remember what we were talking about, but I still remember how it went through me when he said, "Soon you can milk by yourselves." I just stared at him and thought, "What are you going to do?" But I didn't think much about it till after his death. Then it came to my mind again.

We moved to a place that had been neglected for years. Trees had grown along a waterway beside our barn. Martin decided it's time to clean away some of the trees that had branches hanging way out into the field. He asked for my advice about which trees we should leave standing. I felt so uneasy with having him start the dangerous job and I told him so. I felt relieved when all the trees were down and he only had to drag them on a pile.

Our last evening together brings precious memories. We sat up late and enjoyed our time together after the children were in bed, sharing and discussing things on our minds. We could have talked on and on. But Martin was so tired, and I had something to tend to yet. So Martin went to bed and till I got there he was fast asleep. I had thought of something else I wanted to discuss, (not realizing this was our last full day together).

That fateful day started off as any other day, though I remember feeling depressed. Things looked so dark to me, but I couldn't find a good reason to feel that way.

Martin worked in the barn all morning. When he came in for dinner, he said he didn't get everything done in the barn. We sat at the table as a family longer than usual. Then he did some work at the desk. Mahlon (14), our oldest son, and Joseph (12) were talking with him while we did the dishes. Martin paused at the sink to talk a little, never realizing that those would be our last words together.

It didn't seem at all like he realized his life was so near to the end. It is a reminder to us all that we know not the day nor the hour when the Lord calls. If Martin had felt his time was up, he surely would have told me about it.

Martin was dragging trees together on a pile for over an hour. Then Mahlon came running into the house, almost out of breath, and gasped, "Mom, call the ambulance! A tree fell on Dad!"

Oh, the shock that went through me. I started trembling, on the inside anyway, and went right to the phone. I could hardly think to dial. As soon as I was off the phone, I ran out the door. I was halfway out behind the barn before I could see the scene of the accident. Then a feeling of calmness and peace swept through me. A voice seemed to say, "Everything will be all right." When I got to Martin, it didn't look really bad. He was still sitting on the dozer with his hand on the throttle, and his head leaning against a limb. I came up from behind so I didn't see him full in the face. I noticed he was taking deep breaths. A little blood was running down his forehead and nose. That was the only injury I could see.

I heard the ambulance siren when I was halfway out to Martin, so I knew help was on the way. Mahlon asked if he should get the chain saw to cut the limb. He ran for it and started to saw, but then I told him to stop as I realized we shouldn't be doing anything ourselves. I also noticed Martin wasn't really pinched in as the tree had snapped back a little. Afterwards I wished I had tried to say something to him, but the ambulance was almost there. The shop and fence row blocked their view of us, so I ran to the road to direct them.

Mahlon had been fixing something at a silage wagon, as it was about silo-filling time. It wasn't far away from the hedgerow but he couldn't see the dozer from where he was working. Mahlon had heard the dozer running high and went to check what was going on. The limb had knocked the throttle up. I believe Martin had found a limb of a willow tree that he decided to just break off with the dozer blade. With high weeds all around he didn't realize he was so close to the ditch, as it was wider at that point. So when the front end of the dozer blade went down and the limb came up over the dozer and hit his forehead.

The ambulance crew drove right up to where the dozer was. I went to change clothes to go along. When I got back, they ordered me to stay away. They had Martin on a stretcher and were working on him. A policeman told me they plan to take him to the local hospital, then life-flight him to a larger one. It seemed people came from all directions and cars were lined up along the road. A policeman offered to take me to the hospital. Almost right after we got to the hospital, Martin's sister and husband came. (They are the only family members on Martin's or my side living in our community.) Another couple came that lost a son a little over a year before in an accident. One nurse came to me and said everything will be okay. Another said it was bad—really bad! It seemed I was in shock, a blessing at this time, as minds and bodies couldn't handle it all. Oh, what the presence of friends mean at such times! A worker at the hospital offered to take us to the larger hospital. Thus, we began our long hour's drive. It seemed as soon as we reached the hospital, I got the feeling that there isn't much hope for life. I thought about what I had felt at home on the way out to Martin after calling the ambulance. I had taken that feeling to mean he is going to be all right again, but God's ways are far above our ways. Everything is all right when the soul is safe in heaven.

The doctor came to the room where we were waiting and explained to us there is very little hope. But he said,

"Miracles can happen." The reason Martin was still breathing was that the swelling had not reached the part of his brain that controlled the breathing. The doctors said they could put a shunt in to relieve some pressure. We decided to let them do it. I'm glad we did it, so we had the assurance that we had tried everything. I remember thinking, "They don't care, they only want his organs. He's only a farmer to them." They asked if I wanted to see him. Yes, I wanted to go so I could better realize how it was. Oh, the shock to touch his cold, stiff hand that had always been soft before, and to see the gadgets and watch his chest rise and fall unnaturally with the breathing machine. I felt so weak, but there was no place to sit so after shedding tears I left the room. It was now late at night and we were an hour from home so the children didn't get to see Daddy before he died.

We started home in the wee morning hours. The rain, which was coming in torrents, just fitted my feelings. Oh, to come home to seven fatherless children! I talked with each one separately as they woke up. I was surprised they had slept so well. Oh, the shock of the unexpected! I had thought already how it would be if I was left a widow with children, but never really thought it could happen. Always when I thought of death, I thought I'd be the first to go. It just seemed as if the world would stop. But soon I saw everyone else's world went on the same. While watching a neighbor couple walk over in the morning, the realization hit me that Martin and I would never walk together this side of heaven.

Maybe I should write about the many struggles in the months ahead, but I don't really feel like it. Only those who go through grief can comprehend it. I'm sure the grief process is as different as people's personalities.

It meant so much to have most of our family from both sides come the six-hour drive from Pennsylvania that Sunday to help make funeral arrangements. I was glad for all the kind friends and neighbors who also came. Oh, it kept us from feeling so alone. I believe one thing that helped so much is the advice from our bishop and others too. "Take a day at a time and try not to look ahead too much. If you aren't able to see through the day, just take one hour at a time."

The first evening I wondered if I'd be able to sleep. I hadn't slept at all the night of the accident. Martin and I usually read a chapter in the Bible together before we went to bed. That evening the Bible fell open at II Corinthians chapter one. I read, *"Grace be unto you and peace from God, even the Father of mercies and the God of all comfort, who comforteth us in all our tribulations that we may be able to comfort them which are in any trouble, by the comfort where with we ourselves are comforted of God. For as the sufferings of Christ abound in us, so our consolation also aboundeth by Christ. "* This meant so much to me, and probably because of many prayers, I had a good night's rest. The funeral wasn't till Thursday so relatives and friends could come from a distance. Those days dragged but I can't remember much about them. The day of the viewing we had a steady flow of visitors, (several hundred names were recorded in the guest book).

Martin didn't look like himself with his face and lips all swollen. The undertaker didn't want to view, but some friends and family went to the funeral home to decide if he can be viewed. It would have been much harder to realize with a closed coffin.

When Martin's clothes were returned that he had worn when the accident happened, we found his shirt pocket full of notes. He had jotted down things he wanted to remember, also other things he had on his mind.

Lifetime Goals
My three most important long term goals are:
A1 Building a happy, close-knit Christian family
A2 Being a good steward of material possessions
A3 Living to serve others

We also found a typed note he had picked up at a drug store that said, *"You will never find the time for anything. If you want the time, you must make it!"* That's something for all of us to think about.

The day of the funeral, September 30, was a chilly morning. It was hard to believe that it was us this time on the way to church with the funeral procession, always before it had been other people. Oh, the last good-bys for seven children who could have used a Dad. When would a Dad be needed more than now with small children and teenagers? We must try to say, *"Thy will be done."* God makes no mistakes. Will Lois, the youngest, remember her father? She turned three a few days after the funeral. I was so thankful funeral service notes were taken by two different parties. Both did a good job. Did we thank them enough? I hardly would have remembered much as we were so weary and tired from all the stress. Martin had taken notes for a 17-year-old's funeral that was buried at the same church cemetery. It was the last funeral before his. Little did he know he would be next to fill a grave.

The day after the funeral, a lot of neighbors got together and filled our silo. My sister Martha and husband left their dairy herd in someone else's care and stayed for a week to help. Did we thank them properly? Friends and family did so much for us. We could have had a hard struggle without them.

Oh, to go to church the first time without Dad and see his empty place with the song leaders. Oh, the many decisions piled on me. Many times they seemed overwhelming. The responsibilities pushed on such young shoulders to help run a farm... Mahlon soon turned fifteen. A cousin to our children helped us for a year. Mahlon did surprisingly well with managing the feeding. God, in His mercy looked down upon us. For me, the will to work was almost gone. It wasn't hard to do the daily chores of taking care of the family, but I couldn't do much else. We received some flowers after the funeral. I couldn't really enjoy flowers for a long time, but the thought behind those flowers was appreciated.

Seven months after Martin died, a dear little son made his appearance in the family. We named him Martin. This was another responsibility for Mother, but a big sunshine for us all. He was a little gift to cheer us and brighten our days with his sunny cheerfulness. He was a good baby. If he had been fussy, I'd probably have just cried with him. Now several years later he's still such a day-brightener with his cheerful, smiling, and talkative ways.

This evening, little Martin picked up the Bible and said, "This book says, 'God loves me'." Out of the mouth of babes thou hast perfected praise. Yes, God loves us and has well supplied our needs.

—Ella Fox
Penn Yan, New York

DANIEL GEHMAN
February 25, 1953 to March 23, 1992 (39 years)

The Daniel Gehman Family Experience
Janet F. (Gehman) Sauder, Wife

The year of 1991 was the beginning of drastic changes for our family. It was in the fall of that year that Daniel, my husband, started doctoring for what seemed to be an infection in his mouth. A few days before Christmas, they diagnosed him with a lymphoma in his stomach.

Daniel's choice was to visit Mexico for treatment. An anointing service prior to this gave me courage to make the trip, even though his health was already very deteriorated.

We were home from Mexico a few days before Daniel was taken to the hospital by ambulance. Our children, Daniel Jr. (12) and Rosalie (10), had been home-schooled, and continued their studies while in the care of relatives. I spent as much time as I could in the hospital. The support from friends and relatives gave us an overwhelming feeling of unworthiness. It brought to my mind the debt Christ paid for us on the cross, because we owed a debt we could not pay.

During the days and nights in the hospital, I experienced deep "groanings" which could not be uttered. I felt like God's hand lay heavy on us, with the turmoil of the sickness. Daniel's condition often reminded us of Job. He had a rare condition called Steven's Johnson Syndrome which resulted in a skin condition similar to third-degree burns.

These open wounds made cancer treatments impossible. A respirator made it impossible for him to talk, his eyesight was also deteriorating, and he was in a lying position most of the time.

An accountant friend brought a laptop computer which proved to be a Godsend. Even though Daniel could hardly see, he could still type because he had the keyboard memorized. He was an accountant, running his business in the basement of our home. The computer enabled Daniel to give responses to the doctors' and nurses' questions. On one of his better days, he typed a letter of admonition to our two children.

During these days God was gently preparing me to let go. My prayer was, *"Lord, not my will, but Thine be done!"* The thought of possibly facing the future without Daniel seemed overwhelming. But God's grace was always sufficient.

Once I had an uplifting experience that words cannot fully describe. I was leaving the ICU after being with Daniel, and the burden of the unknown future was weighing heavily on me. As I entered the ICU waiting room, I noticed an oriental man seated in one of the chairs. He acknowledged my entrance and spoke some words of encouragement. I immediately felt my burden was lightened. But when I turned to smile and thank him, there was no one there. I was awed by the reality of God's presence in the room. The feeling of deep reverence that filled me cannot be described. God's timing is always perfect.

After a three-month illness, the death angel appeared on March 23, 1992, which was the day of our daughter Rosalie's eleventh birthday. Again it seemed too sacred for words, this miracle of death. As I entered Daniel's room after all medical instruments were removed, he looked so peaceful. Suddenly it felt like such hallowed ground that the thought struck me, "The Master was just here." The feeling was so strong that I glanced around the room, thinking I could catch a glimpse of the Lord.

At the burial scene, my grief was too deep to be expressed by tears. It started to rain heavily and I was touched by the thought that God was weeping for me. I was reminded again of His infinite love.

Looking back, I see only one set of footprints. We were indeed both carried by the Heavenly Father, and He continued to carry me in the days that followed, in funeral preparations and many decisions. He was indeed a husband to me and a father to our children. The Lord showed Himself strong while I was going *through* the valley of grief. I found He is indeed a widow's God. I absorbed myself in the scriptures, and talked to the Lord constantly. Books that were given to me that I found a great comfort in are *A Shepherd Looks At Psalm 23* by Philip Keller, *Streams In The Desert* by Mrs. Charles Cowman, and *Daily Light From The Bible* by Barbour and Company, Inc.

I felt the Lord's provision through people in innumerable ways. I thanked the Lord for lending Daniel for the amount of time He did, and for the enrichment Daniel's influence had on my life and on others. *"... the Lord gave, and the Lord hath taken away; blessed be the name of the Lord"* (Job 1:21b).

More trials came in November of the same year with the death of my father.

> *My ways, my child are not your ways,*
> *My thoughts are higher than thine.*
> *Let me lead you each step of this long weary day,*
> *Let me clasp thy trembling hand in Mine.*
> *-M. Nichols*

(Found in the *Expanded Practical Music Reader.*)

Two-and-one-half years later a widower from our area, Leroy Sauder, asked for my friendship. The night before he called, I wrestled in prayer for several hours until I found peace. I received the assurance that, should God's will be that I remarried, His grace would be sufficient for what He asked me to bear. Even though I had no idea that anyone was planning to call, it seemed like the Lord was preparing me for this. When Leroy's call came, I spent much time in prayer and fasting, again seeking the Lord's will. I thought it would take a long time for me to decide what my answer would be, but in a short time God revealed that I should go forward in faith, trusting in His sufficient grace.

My prayer is that this story will honor God, our only steadfast hope. As Daniel said of his sickness, "That God be glorified through it all."

—*Janet F. Sauder*
Ephrata, Pennsylvania

Be assured that,
regardless of where you are,
what you are doing,
or what you are going through,
God, in all things and in all ways,
is doing the most loving thing
concerning you.

-Roy Lessin

ANGUS MARTIN
November 7, 1951 to October 22, 1982 (30 years)

The Everlasting Arms
Leah Martin, Wife

"The eternal God is thy refuge and underneath are the everlasting arms" (Deuteronomy 33:27).

It was exceptionally clear and sunny that memorable day, October 22, 1982, and these were the last words anybody heard my husband, Angus Martin say: "Nice day today." Yes, for him it was a very nice day.

The men had just finished cutting corn in their big round, and we were so glad to have Dad at home again more during the day. Especially three-and-one-half year-old Elo, who was his father's shadow since he was a toddler. I remember clearly one morning both came in and as we were discussing something Elo began copying Dad's position, leaning on the counter top with one hand and balancing his one foot on the other, the same as his dad. What a team! He had long days when his dad was gone during the day for his sister Anna (6) had started to school in September. His younger sister Sarah, at 20 months, was a little young to make a good playmate yet, although they did have many happy times together. Our life was complete—or so we thought.

Two-and-one-half weeks prior to this memorable day, dark clouds started gathering in our sky. I could sense something was on my husband's mind and waited till he was ready to share. One evening he expressed his desire for deeper, lasting peace. We prayed earnestly for help in this matter and our answer came while we were still in prayer. I will not go into detail here of the experience, but my husband received a deep peace that night. When discussing it afterward I told him, "I don't understand what it all means but I am ready to commit myself to God's will whatever it is." Without hesitating he said he feels it means he will die soon, even though he had not seen the vision.

A stab went through my heart and it was the beginning of a weight gathering there that did not get less as the days went by. Still I tried to convince myself one does not really know when the time comes to die.

After this Angus had a deep desire and burden for everyone to have this peace while there is still time. He found he could not join the light-hearted banter the last while when a group was together and tended rather to become withdrawn and quiet. At night he would unburden his heart and pray for friends and loved ones and our small family. I cherish many of our talks we had that last while, sometimes late into the night. Our last night together our devotions lasted a long time and he talked a lot about heaven. He also quoted the benediction in German and I so well remember the look on his face as if each word held special meaning for him.

I rejoiced to see the deep joy Angus now possessed, but found as his joy ran deeper, my load increased. One morning after breakfast I came out to the barn to bring him a message and found him up in the pig barn, leaning on a fork, his face uplifted with a faraway look in his eyes. I will never forget the look of radiance on his face and it smote my heart again. A few sacred moments as all was still, even the pigs. My husband was being borne to a realm of which I was not a part. Then he turned his face and his eyes met mine. Instantly they held a look of pain. Maybe they mirrored the pain in my own eyes. We needed no words. Life was still going on.

My husband was a hard worker, but he always had time for his family. Even though earthly things held little value to him now, he was in earnest to get everything in order. He would explain many things to me and with a sinking feeling I tried to gather it all in. The day before he left, I asked him if we want to get all our records in the barn on paper as so much he just stored in his head. He was willing but we did not get around to it that day, as it was nice out and he wanted to get some outdoor work done.

We had a maid, Maryann Martin, for that summer which meant a lot to us as my back was giving me some trouble. That morning I had an appointment in Fergus and went with the bus which passed our lane. On the way home I was hoping my husband would still be in the house when I got home, but realized they would probably be finished eating and he would be outside again. I had heard the words from my chiropractor that we weren't sure we would ever hear. He said, "In six weeks your back will be healed if you don't do any work in that time." My maid was leaving the next week and I couldn't see how we'd manage.

Coming in the door, I rejoiced to see them still at the table. I treasured this meal together and shared what was on my mind. As usual my husband thought there would be a way through, although I could not see it yet. Little did I know...

After dinner I headed for the couch. Angus came in shortly afterward and said he is going over to his parents, Aaron and Salome Martin, to fix a small part on the loader with the welder. He wondered if I needed some bulk groceries. We talked a bit more and he still lingered. He asked if there's anything else, and I couldn't think of anything more to share and said, "I don't want to keep you up any longer." I don't think we said "good-by," but our eyes held.

I promptly fell into a deep sleep and had a hard time waking up when Maryann came in asking questions about the garden. Shortly thereafter Irvin Frey's daughter, Miriam, who was at Aaron's at the time also, came in the door all out of breath. She said Angus had been in a bad accident and I am supposed to come right away. I asked if someone called the ambulance and she said Grandma Salome went to the neighbors to call and also sent messages to the married children living nearby to come right away. Angus' sister Adeline went back to Lukes' farm where Aaron and two teenage sons, Luke and James were working.

I grabbed my coat, bonnet, and purse still lying on the table and started running, hoping I'd get over before the ambulance came. We have a back lane leading over to their farm and as I reached the far side of the garden a voice seemed to say, "Don't run. The rush is past." I gasped and wondered, "Did he already die?" The answer came again, "Yes, I called him Home." I stopped short, the truth soaking in. One-by-one like pages in a book the memories flipped through my mind backward till the book was closed. I felt myself sinking under the blow. How can I go on? Half of my heart died with him. The other half was ripped open. But no, what is this? Slowly deep peace flooded my soul and flowed through my bleeding heart. Oh, the strength and comfort of the Everlasting Arms! The strength of a widow's God was already there as soon as it was needed.

Slowly I walked on over, my heart light, and instead of the weight—deep abiding peace. I was very thankful neither the children nor I had to be the first to find him. I was not imagining a very pleasant sight if the loader came down on his head. (The sparks had ruptured the oil hoses.) But I felt

I had to go over and hear someone say my husband had passed away.

I met Angus' Mother first, although the others were quickly gathering, too. I sensed an urgency I did not feel. The look of shock on Grandma's face told me something drastic had happened, so I asked her, "Did he die?" She took me in her arms, but I still needed to hear the words. I looked up to her face and asked again, and she nodded numbly. Then I knew what my heart already knew. My husband had died. There was a longing to try and break the news to my children before too many people came. There was lots of help here and my husband didn't need me anymore.

I was home on my knees trying to tell my three-year-old son his Dad had gone to heaven when my mother-in-law came over. Afraid the shock might almost be too much for her, I suggested she lie on the couch, which she did. After what seemed like a long time, some more family members came over. Aaron went along up to the hospital with the ambulance. Some time later a policeman came to the door with some questions. Grandma Salome went to answer them, which I appreciated. He asked if we knew about the accident, and I think he realized he had come to the house of mourning as we were all wearing black. I also learned Angus hardly had a mark on him when they lifted the loader. Just a small dent on his one temple. Hope rose within as I realized we would be able to see his form again anyway. My prayers go out to all those who don't have this privilege.

We decided not to fetch Anna at school as they were having their much looked-forward-to fall party. When the school bus came I went out to meet her. She was older and her feelings ran deeper. We both cried when I told her, "Dad has gone to heaven." She knew her life here had changed forever. Elo still had to learn over and over again that his dad would not come back to live with us. Sarah in her innocence did not fully realize what was happening and often was a ray of sunshine in the coming days.

By now my parents, Nelson and Sarah Brubacher, had received the word of the accident, too. Angus was discovered around 2:30 and some time elapsed before they were allowed to send out word. My parents received the word at 5:30 from kind neighbors. One brother and two sisters were still living at home. My oldest sister, Valina, had a weight pressing in her heart which also lifted now. My father had a grave heart condition at the time and as it got later and later that evening the others tried to tell me maybe it would be too much to make the 45 miles that evening. I continued to watch the window and when I saw headlights coming in the lane, my hope rose. I had to see my mother! When she came in, we fell into each others arms, tears and love flowed. How precious to have my parents! Brother Amsey and his wife Karen brought them. The look of love and peace on Karen's face and her three words, "Keep looking up" was just what I needed. Many more were the words of comfort and encouragement before and after the funeral.

The sermon at the funeral also was like a balm to the broken heart. Oh how many blessings we still do have even if all around the future looks dark. How true, we only need to take one step at a time.

I wish I could say this peace continued but I could not sleep. This took its toll and I needed help. Through this dark valley I could still pray and feel God's love. I knew Satan is mighty, but God is Almighty. After my mind was healed again, I thanked God daily for sound sleep. It was several months before I could sleep without medication.

Valina came to help us and was a wonderful support. Hired help was also found to do the farm work and by God's grace and people's generous help we are still able to live here. After 14 years of hired help my son Elo took over the responsibilities. Sarah is also at home, and Anna married Amon Martin in 1997. Baby Nelson has come to join them bringing much joy as well.

Several years after Valina came to help us, she married David Shantz in 1985 and also moved to a farm in this area. Ten years after Angus was called Home we went through all this again when also after seven-and-one-half years of marriage Valina's husband, David, died after a very short illness. He left his wife and three sons ages six, four, and almost two. It was also the end of October, but in 1992. Once again God's love carried us through; but how it hurt to see my own sister, who did so much for me, walk the valley of sorrow.

A year later in October 1993, Aaron Martin, Angus' father, was killed instantly when the front part of his carriage broke when he was taking his grandchildren to school. Sarah (12) was the oldest and ran for help while the youngest ones huddled together at the end of a driveway until help arrived. Aaron was thrown out onto the road, protecting the children as they were thrown against him. Yes, once again God had reached down and taken Home a loved one. We trust Father and son are now together again and although we do not always understand God's ways, we know He makes no mistakes.

-Leah Martin
Kenilworth, Ontario, Canada

Earth has lost its look of gladness.
Heaven seems to us more bright,
Since the spirit of our loved ones
Took their happy homeward flight.

Just as the falling of the leaves
That flutter in the autumn breeze
Softly, drifting to the ground
Silently, without a sound.

October—it has come again—bringing tears like falling rain. Once more we stand at a grave side, and the doors of memory open wide! Eleven years have passed between... Oh, how long—yet, how short they seem. Again our hearts are plunged in grief. Can we somewhere find relief from the shadow of this sorrow that has been hung over tomorrow?
But wait—for now we can dimly see the light that still shines endlessly! And we can feel from deep within—a touch—and know that it is Him who saw it best to give another loved one rest. Although we do not understand, we know it is as God has planned.

-Elsie Martin, Sister of Leah

DAVID HOOVER
October 18, 1956 to July 19, 1991 (34 years)

The Lord Provides
Ellen Hoover, Wife

We were a very busy, happy, young family that year of 1991. We had moved to a New York dairy farm from our native state of Pennsylvania exactly one year after our March 1979 wedding. I distinctly remember walking in from the barn one evening with our six children ranging in ages from eight years to seven months. When suddenly the thought struck me, "What would I do if I had to go on alone? Well, I guess I would sell the cows," was my first thought. But then I quickly pushed all such thoughts out of my mind. Little did I realize how soon they would become reality. As I think back over this incident, I believe it was the voice of God preparing me somewhat for the tragedy I would soon experience.

It was a hot, sultry day in July when we were expecting my brother and family to come from Pennsylvania. They were coming to our community for a wedding the next day. I had done the milking alone that evening as David was busy baling hay. I had finished the milking and was starting to wash up when one of the children shouted that a calf was loose. From there on I remember nothing. I will just write it as people have told me. David came home with a load of hay just then. We had a merry chase trying to catch the calf. When she tried to jump a drainage hole that was covered with a thin plywood board, the board broke dumping the calf into the hole which was approximately eight feet deep. It was partly filled with waste water and chemicals from the washup after evening milking. We had been having trouble with a clogged drain pipe, and David had been working on it which was the reason why it wasn't covered with something more permanent. David stuck a ladder down into the hole trying to rescue the calf, never realizing the danger of harmful fumes being present. He was overcome by the fumes and fell to the bottom. I then went down the ladder to help David. About that time my brother, Luke Zimmerman from Pennsylvania arrived. Hearing the children's shouts, they were soon on the scene. Luke secured a rope around himself and went in to get me out. After giving me artificial respiration and seeing that I was breathing again, they got David out. But since he was in longer than I was, life had already fled.

I spent the next two weeks in the hospital, being unconscious about half the time. I am sure God heard the many prayers of my family and church, because He chose to heal me. Chemical pneumonia had set in from the toxic fumes I had breathed in. Physically I recovered quite rapidly, but the emotional healing of losing my partner was much slower.

God was with me every step of the way and slowly but surely, I recovered. I wonder if my grief wasn't more drawn-out as I never experienced the funeral. I believe my hardest moment was the first night I was home from the hospital. My sister-in-law had come to stay with me and the children. After they had all retired for the night, I sat at the kitchen table reading a bit before I went to bed. I had often done that before, waiting till David would come in from the barn. This time he did not come in, and the full realization struck me—he is gone!

The barns were all so silent, as the cows had all been sold. The bank had more or less made that decision as we had money borrowed from them for the cows. No one knew whether I would recover, or how soon. I feel it was the best thing to do as the cows were in very good shape yet and brought quite a good price. With different people doing the milking and feeding, the cows might have developed more health problems. I am glad I was not conscious when that decision was made, as I would not have been emotionally fit to make it myself. I enjoyed working outside and in the barn, but my children were too small yet to be a lot of help. The two oldest girls were in first and second grade and the four boys were all preschoolers. There was no one of the family that could have taken over as a hired hand, so the decision was made to sell the farm and equipment.

I would like to mention here, I don't think I would have been able to survive such a tremendous upheaval in my life, had it not been for the many willing hands and support I received from my family and friends of the church. I was flooded with mail and visitors, sometimes almost overwhelmingly.

The decision of, "What do I do now?" was of major concern and took much thought and prayer. My family mostly all lived in Pennsylvania, but there the homes were much higher priced and it was more crowded. I loved the quieter and more open spaces and we wanted to raise our family on the farm. Without the support of my husband, I leaned more heavily on my Lord. After much prayer the way seemed to be opening up. I found a smaller farm close to some of our church families. It had a rundown barn but a fairly large house. It was more acres than I wanted, but that was soon taken care of with neighbors happy to rent some of the land. Another question was settled when a dairyman came to me, wondering if I would want to raise his calves. He was having trouble keeping them alive. This seemed to be just the thing to provide some work for the children and was something I enjoyed and was familiar with. It has proven successful and I have expanded my work, adding more calf hutches and putting up another barn so I can raise bigger calves and heifers.

We have also tried selling some produce as the children are getting older and need more to keep them busy. This is an area I can expand in as well.

There are always young families needing help, and I am happy to let the children help out at other homes as the need arises. I feel it is good for the children, too. Especially the boys, as they do not have a father to copy.

The Lord has certainly been gracious by providing for me in a way I did not think possible.

—Ellen Hoover
Waterloo, New York

"Now our Lord Jesus Christ himself, and God, even our Father, which hath loved us, and hath given us everlasting consolation and good hope through grace, Comfort your hearts, and stablish you in every good word and work (IIThessalonians 2:16-17).

WELDON R. ZIMMERMAN
August 31, 1951 to January 8, 1995 (43 years)

The Midnight Call
Reba M. Zimmerman, Wife

"Trust in the Lord with all thine heart; and lean not unto thine own understanding. In all thy ways acknowledge him and he shall direct thy paths" (Proverbs 3:5-6).

Excitement was in the air on March 3, 1980. Our family of six: Weldon, Reba (myself), Duane (8), Kathryn (6), Galen (3), Rosalie (18 months), was anticipating our move from Elkhart, Indiana to Decker, Michigan. There we had bought a run-down dairy farm. Oh, what an enjoyable time we had cleaning and fixing it up in the next few years.

We were one of a group of six Wisler Mennonite families to purchase farms in this new community and settle there that spring. We were a small but close-knit group beginning our church and Christian day school. Years rolled by and the group gradually grew and increased in number. Our family also increased. Jeremy arrived in 1984 and two years later Aaron was born.

Ten years after our move, Weldon had his first sign of serious health problems on Sunday, March 4, 1990, when he had a grand maul seizure. He had always been bothered with headaches but other than that he had lived a life free from health problems. The headaches had been more frequent and more severe as the years passed. He didn't realize what was taking place until after he found out he had a brain tumor.

That first seizure came on Sunday. His headache was bad, but he attended church as usual. He remarked he should get his eyes checked. He had trouble seeing the ministers that day because of double vision and he felt like someone had slapped his eyes hard. By evening he felt he had the flu and left the barn early, leaving the children to finish up the chores. This was very unusual for him. He had a low-grade fever, felt upset to his stomach, and a general aching feeling all over.

Duane and Kathryn had left for singing and the rest of us went to bed early. Later, I was awakened by a strange noise and odd breathing sounds from Weldon. My thoughts immediately flew to possible heart problems as his dad had just recently had a five-by-pass heart surgery. I immediately called for an ambulance. I also called my sister, Esther and Donald Martin. They came as soon as possible. I was so thankful to have someone with me that night. We called the children at singing and asked them to come home so the little ones weren't alone while we went to the hospital.

Then began the ordeal at the hospital of asking and answering questions and running tests. Three days later came the shocking blow. The CAT scan showed Weldon had a brain tumor. Things quickly proceeded toward surgery. He was transferred to a larger hospital 45 minutes away. Surgery was scheduled for five days later, March 12, 1990.

We were well aware of some effects of brain tumors and brain surgeries as Weldon had a friend from Indiana, Minister Merle Ramer, who had undergone surgery for a brain tumor. So we didn't feel like pioneers, and yet the struggle to accept this was overwhelming and the future looked bleak.

Life at home had suddenly changed. Where Dad had been in control, the children's responsibilities now increased. Duane (17) was suddenly in charge of the farm, and Kathryn (15) quit school to become "Mom" to the two little boys while I spent time with Dad at the hospital.

Our church families and neighbors helped with food and chores whenever needed. They have always been here when needed, then and now. It is very humbling to be on the receiving end.

The night before surgery, sleep would not come for me as I struggled to let God have full control of Weldon's life. I felt I needed him so badly to help raise these little ones the Lord had blessed us with. Through the tears, prayers, and God's Word, He gave a calm reassurance and I was reminded once again, no matter what is to come, He is with me each step I take. God's way is best.

Surgery day came and so did many family members, friends and ministers from here in Michigan and also Indiana. Each one shared words of comfort, encouragement, and prayers.

The surgery went as well as could be expected. The tumor was operated on, removing all that they could at 80 per cent. It was found to be a malignant, low-grade right frontal astrocytoma, (a slow-growing cancer), on the right side of his brain. Weldon lost some use of his left side which therapy helped bring back. No treatments were required and he was told he could live five to ten years, or even a normal life span.

A few days later came another blow when he began to seizure. Seizure medication now became a way of life while going from doctor to doctor trying to curb the seizures. Weldon was soon back home again to the farm and family he loved. He never learned to enjoy waiting in doctors' offices or hospitals.

The next four years were fairly good years. His seizure medication was changed often and dosages were adjusted quite frequently. But the seizures continued varying in intensity and frequency. Weldon had always enjoyed working with his hands. But now things had certainly changed, forcing him to slow down, and taking time to "smell the roses". We spent more time doing things together as a family. Although life was not without difficulties, Weldon accepted the change of losing his freedom of being able to operate or drive the farm equipment, to hop into a vehicle and to go to town for parts, to letting others take the driver's seat because of seizures. All these were hard pills to swallow. On several occasions, Weldon actually climbed into the combine with one of the children and operated the machine himself.

We depended greatly on the children and those in the community to keep the farm going. Jeremy and Aaron followed their daddy around everywhere he would go so if he'd have a seizure they were there to help him, or to run for help if needed.

We all worked together on some special projects. The first project was adding onto our house in 1993. We also accomplished another rewarding project in our backyard. This we termed as our "Therapy Garden." It is a large flower garden with paths and fish ponds. We have a plaque in the garden which reads:

Father
You were always there
  with loving care
Through good times and
  through bad
You guided me with strength and love
  You were the perfect Dad.

There is also a rock in the garden which has inscribed on it: *"An hour in the garden puts life's problems in perspective."* I'd like to change it to read, *"Being with the Lord in the Therapy Garden puts life's problems in perspective."*

May 1994 we were anxiously looking forward to Weldon's next checkup as we felt he was showing significant signs of trouble. There was an increase of seizures, headaches, pressure behind his eyes, weakening of his left side, and just not feeling well, all symptoms we had seen before. The doctor assured us things were okay. But yet she set up an appointment for an MRI in July, then turned to Weldon and said, "You know, Weldon, someday your brain tumor will probably give you trouble again." This surprised us as always before she had been really upbeat, assuring us things were fine.

Back home again, things weren't going well, and Weldon was always tired. I thought it was just the stress on Weldon of getting the farm work done. Finally, I felt we needed to do something as Weldon could no longer rationalize at times, making it very difficult for everyone. The children had been taught how the chores should be done, and now sometimes Dad's advice just didn't make sense.

We began to plan for a vacation. Our plan was for the three older children to stay at home and help with the chores while I take Weldon and the younger three children on a trip. (Now I regret that we didn't take all the children along, as this was Dad's last vacation on this earth.) We headed East, taking time to let Weldon relax and rest as needed. We visited a few friends and relatives and did some sightseeing. The trip really didn't improve Weldon's health. In fact, till we got home, he was having more and harder seizures, and was using a cane to walk.

We were soon at Ann Arbor for the scheduled MRI and were then told the tumor was growing again and it had fingers reaching into his brain. Their plan this time was for a series of 35 radiation treatments. During those treatments we lived in Ann Arbor week days and drove home to be with the family for Saturday and Sunday. This wasn't an easy time for any of us, but it taught us many lessons in patience. We learned to trust and take just one day at a time, step-by-step.

Then followed two months when Weldon was more like his old self. The children learned to know Dad as I had known him. They heard him laugh his hardy, rolling laugh like I had known it.

Just before Thanksgiving Weldon came down with pneumonia, putting him in the hospital again. He began to seizure harder and for longer periods of time, leaving his left side almost useless. We took him back to Ann Arbor, this time using a wheel chair instead of a cane. They did a CAT scan which showed the tumor was larger and growing. The doctor told us his days are numbered and they could do no more. At that, Weldon just sighed and sat back. He finally knew the fight was over. They stated that his left side was definitely weaker and his tumor was growing. We were told to go home and make him comfortable. Later, the doctors apologized for not telling us, in the spring, that they sensed his problems came from the tumor. They gave us a copy of that earlier appointment.

Weldon was at peace and just patiently waited, enduring pain and suffering, till the Lord called him home.

On December 1, we got him a hospital bed, setting it up in the dining room where he could be one of us and in the center of activity, where he could see out the windows toward the barn and the road. He rested better with his head elevated, but we did need to place foam cushions under the legs of his bed. Otherwise, he felt the vibrations in his head as people walked across the floor. Hospice sent nurses out to help wherever and whenever they could. They kept his medications regulated keeping him fairly comfortable. Those last days seemed to go on and on. But looking back, I realize it was so short.

Family members came in to stay with Weldon at night. On Friday, January 6, he began asking for his mom. That evening his parents arrived from Indiana. As his mom stood at his beside, he held her hand and said, "Mama." As an infant this was probably the first word his lips tried, and now it was his last.

Saturday, the seventh, his eyes followed us around the room but as the day wore on his body slowly began shutting down. Here lay my husband of twenty-three years looking like an old man, and dying. At 9:00 p.m. the family, and those who were here at the time, stood around his bed. We sang, read Psalm 23, and prayed closing with the Lord's Prayer. Weldon tried to help say the Lord's Prayer.

His brother Paul took the first shift that night. While sitting at Weldon's bedside, Paul noticed Weldon seemed restless, so he read from the Bible for a while. This calmed Weldon. Then while resting he realized Weldon was breathing differently. So he called us and we all gathered around his bed as a family, where we watched him pass away so quietly and peacefully. It was a blessing to be able to witness his going.

At that moment, someone glanced at the clock, and both hands were straight up—it was midnight. thus came the thought of the song, "Are you ready for the midnight call?" Here was a new day—a day of rest—Sunday morning January 8, 1995 and Weldon could now finally rest. He would have no more seizures, no more pain, no more suffering, no more death.

God's timing is perfect! God had spared husband and Dad almost five more years—years of added growth for the children. Duane (22) was the oldest, down to Aaron (8) who was the youngest. We tried to prepare for the day Dad would leave us behind. He helped guide the four oldest into the fold, and witnessed their baptisms. Those last weeks his mind often went to those who seemed to be slipping in the faith and then to his own two little boys coming on behind that they too may someday come into the fold.

The visitations and funeral were all held at the funeral parlor in Sandusky, Michigan. Our new church building was still in the planning stages and the present one was too small for the funeral services. Our hearts were deeply touched by the many caring friends and relatives who ventured out in the cold of winter to be with us.

Weldon's final resting place was the first grave at the site of the new church, out in an open field seeming so harsh and cold and lonely. That summer the new church was erected. Also, my sister, Esther and Donald Martin, moved the grave of their eleven-year-old son from a township cemetery to rest beside Weldon's grave.

In July came the marriage of our daughter Kathryn to Kendall Shaum of Indiana. The wedding ceremony and reception were held here at home as Weldon had helped plan it. This was one of those firsts that may come in the life of the bereft. And now I was alone without Weldon's support, yet feeling blessed somehow.

Kendall and Kathryn now have four children—precious little grandchildren whom I often hug a little tighter thinking how Weldon would have loved them. He loved children so!

In the years since Weldon's death I have gone through the afflictions of a mental disorder which the doctors have termed as Bi-Polar depression. During this time, and through it all, the Lord has been by my side. Although I now look back at those times when my mind couldn't grasp life, except on an unrealistic realm, I am embarrassed at some things and actions I said and helplessly done. I praise the Lord! He has led me through and my prayers remain as always, that He could somehow use all my mistakes and victories to His honor and glory, and that I can learn all He has for me to learn.

This has been my theme verse: *"They that wait upon the Lord shall renew their strength; they shall mount up with wings as eagles; they shall run and not be weary, they shall walk and not faint"* (Isaiah 40:31).

All this has been especially hard for my children. I thank the Lord for each one of them as they have stood by me making it easier to bear. I thank the Lord for allowing the medical field to advance in the treatment of illnesses of the mind. That knowledge allows people to live normal lives with proper medications the same as any other illnesses of the body such as high blood pressure, etc.

Yes, sad to say, there is still the stigma of early years when mental illnesses were something "hush-hush" and put severe cases away in institutions. Many people felt there was a spiritual problem as the cause, which is not always the case just as any other illness.

During Weldon's bout with brain cancer, and now later my illness, I marvel at God's unique working of the human brain which is so intricately made.

The worst struggle I had was to accept the fact I was sick, and then to find out I would be on medication the rest of my life for a mental disorder. Family support and dedicated Christian counselors have helped me so much.

This has been very difficult for me to write all this, knowing I am baring my innermost struggles, but I do this with the thought, if just one person can find comfort in knowing they are not alone, and can get the help they need, it will be worth it all. There is light ahead and comfort is ever-present in the storm.

All things work together for good to them that love God.

—*Reba Zimmerman*
Decker, Michigan

My Need

Lord give me a faith that trusts in thee,
For the way is dark; I cannot see.
A faith that clings to the Savior's hand,
When life becomes hard to understand;
That has learned to smile, through tear-filled eyes,
And keep pressing onward for the prize.
When plans have failed and hope's grown dim
I need a faith that can REST in Him.

-Author Unknown

ELAM KRAEMER
August 10, 1941 to January 5, 1969 (27 years)

Heaven Will Surely Be Worth It All

Almeda (Kraemer) Martin, Wife

"For my thoughts are not your thoughts, neither are your ways my ways, saith the Lord. For as the heavens are higher than the earth, so are my ways higher than your ways, and my thoughts than your thoughts" (Isaiah 55:8-9).

On December 11, 1962, Elam and I joined hands in matrimony. We settled on a farm with visions and plans for the future, not thinking that our marriage would only be for six short years. On Nov. 9, 1963, we had a stillborn son. Two-and-a-half years later on April 13, 1966, we had a stillborn daughter. It was hard not to question why, especially when another couple had twins. God's ways are not our ways. We wanted to accept God's way. I felt if I need to go through this again, I could, if it brings God still closer. Little did I realize what lay ahead. With little hope of having a family of our own, we desired to open our home to the homeless. About a year later an eight-week-old boy, whom we named Floyd, came into our hearts and lives.

Life continued on with its ups and downs. One day Elam said, "I don't think I'll become old." I thought, "Are you serious?" Later another morning he said, "Last night I dreamed we had auction sale and the machinery was lined up in the field beside the road." (This later became a fact.) Again I questioned, but his remark soon left me. God doesn't want us to dwell on these phrases when they happen, but they are as comforting thoughts later.

New Years Day 1969 was a very stormy day. The car got stuck in the snow at the end of the lane. Elam decided to shovel it out before chore time. After a while I looked out the window and through the storm I could see him just standing there, facing the storm. I wondered, "What does he see?" Later in the house I longed to ask, but something kept me from doing so. The next three days were precious days, but something loomed in the air.

Sunday, January 5, death knocked on our door. We couldn't go to church as the car wouldn't shift into reverse for there was ice and snow packed in the shifting linkage area. Later Elam decided he could get the ice and snow out and we could go visit a cousin. After spending some time reading and playing with Floyd, Elam got up and said he should go. He got dressed and went to the door, turned and looked at us, then went out the door and out of our lives. I was rather restless and wandered aimlessly around the kitchen. After awhile, I put dinner on the stove. At times I glanced out the window toward the shed. Sometime later the dog howled. I looked out. The dog was sitting beside the shed, and again it howled, such a pitiful howl. I sensed something was wrong out there and need to go and check. So I bundled up, left Floyd in the house, and headed for the shed. I felt a Presence with me. As I neared the shed, something told me to keep calm. I looked in, and behold, the big handyman jack had slipped, crushing Elam. I reached for his leg. It was limp. Something told me life is gone. Death seemed to have been instant. Was there no time to cry, "God be merciful to me a sinner?" He wasn't perfect and failed as humans do.

What should I do now? Floyd was alone. I trudged toward the house and found him playing in the kitchen. Needing help, I phoned cousin Melvin, who lived up the road. No answer. I phoned Wilmer, another neighbor. A girl answered and said they'd send help. Soon three or four neighbors came, and I went out again. One of them jacked up the car, then Wilmer grabbed Elam's legs and pulled him out. I can still hear him say, "Bova, es is fahtich!" English translation, "Boys, it's finished!" One of the men went with me to the house to make phone calls. I found Floyd contentedly playing. (I like to think an unseen angel was with him, as usually he cried after me when I went out the door.)

As the afternoon slowly wore on, relatives and neighbors came. In the evening, as a minister was leaving, he said to me, "Vell, no gabsht dich grod uf." (Just give up yourself.) This almost stabbed my heart some more, as I wanted to hear comforting words. But it was exactly what I needed, as that was exactly what I had to do, hard though it was. How often those words helped me in the following days and years.

During the viewing, a lady said to be sure to touch Elam's hand, it helps to give them up. That evening after callers left, I went alone into the room. I laid my hand on his and felt a slight move as if the knuckle in the forefinger moved to say "come." I stepped back, awe-struck. After I composed myself, I couldn't resist doing it again, then only did I feel the coldness. No words can express the touch of God's hand and presence. Death is so final. After battling with the thought, "Was he truly ready?" I now had peace.

The morning of the funeral dawned bright and clear. The weather had been stormy the day before and after. That morning I pleaded to God for extra strength to face the day. I opened the Bible at random. Here was a picture of Christ praying at the mount of Olives before his crucifixion, and underneath were the words from St. Luke, *"And he came out, and went, as he was wont, to the mount of Olives; and his disciples also followed him. And when he was at the place he said unto them, pray that ye enter not into temptation. And he was withdrawn from them about a stone's cast, and kneeled down, and prayed, saying Father, if thou be willing, remove this cup from me. Nevertheless not my will, but thine, be done. And there appeared an angel unto him from heaven, strengthening him"* (St. Luke 22:39-43). With renewed strength and my hand in the Lord's, I was carried through another day.

I had imagined people thinking, such an unwise and foolish thing to do, to crawl under a jacked-up car. At the funeral service a minister mentioned something similar. He then related a few incidents. One man was hit and killed while riding a bicycle. Another man was struck down by lightning while walking across the field. He went on to say. "Should we not ride a bike? Should we not walk across the field?" Then he remarked, "Dear Christian friends, we cannot escape death!"

People react to shock and emotion in various ways. Some can shed tears freely. Others cannot. If we can't, we may feel people must think we don't care. Deep inside we are crying, but without tears. It was one of those nights while tucking Floyd into bed that he again asked, "Where is Daddy?" How do you explain to a twenty-two-month-old child that his daddy died? That night after all was dark and quiet, the floodgates opened and the tears could flow. We need to release our emotions so healing can begin.

When I had read those words in St. Luke 22, "Pray that ye enter not into temptation," I felt it doesn't apply to me, since God's presence seemed so close at the time. How could Satan tempt me? But, my friends, he can and does tempt us. After awhile, he'll try to tempt us with self-pity or discouragement. We need God's help to stay above these circumstances.

Another lesson I needed to learn was to be a graceful receiver, as so many friends wanted to give or do something. Thanks to them all!

We all have a purpose in life, be it long or short. The death of loved ones can be stepping stones in our Christian life, if we let it.

—*Almeda (Kraemer) Martin*
Listowel, Ontario

"*But I rejoiced in the Lord greatly, that now at the last your care of me hath flourished again; wherein ye were also careful, but ye lacked opportunity. Not that I speak in respect of want: for I have learned, in whatsoever state I am, therewith to be content. I know both how to be abased, and I know how to abound: every where and in all things I am instructed both to be full and to be hungry, both to abound and to suffer need. I can do all things through Christ which strengtheneth me. Notwithstanding ye have well done, that ye did communicate with my affliction* (Philippians 4:10-14).

BARBARA (BRUBACHER) MARTIN
October 6, 1949 to February 22, 1973 (23 years)

Till Death Do Us Part
Leonard Martin, Husband

On May 25, 1971, Barbara and I were married. We stayed at her parents place overnight, with plans to leave the next morning for a short wedding trip. The next morning after breakfast as we shook hands and said good-by to each member of the family, we noticed Barbara's only sister Marion was weeping. In our joy of starting a new home, we did not think of the sadness of parting. These two sisters were very close to each other and did a lot of singing together. Even though we made our home 40 miles from their place, we still planned to keep close contact. I stored this incident in my memory, wondering if it might have more meaning than we realized.

The next spring on April 6, 1972, Marion married Melvin Brubacher. On June 7, 1972, Marlene was born into our home.

Melvin's paid us a visit in January 1973. Before they left, we offered them a pair of baby shoes that we had left over, as they were expecting their first child soon. They didn't know if they should accept them. Then they shared with us that a dark cloud, which does not want to go away, is hanging over them. What does it mean? Will their child not live?

On Feb. 21, 1973, Barbara had planned to go to her parents for the day. But that morning it was snowing, so much so that she did not want to drive. So it was decided to leave it. Maybe tomorrow it will be nicer. The next morning it had stopped snowing, so it was decided she would go. She called her parents to say she was planning to come for the day. Her brother Laverne, answered the phone and I think he was the last one to talk to her. I had already left for Wroxeter to unload a trailer load of fertilizer at our warehouse. Barbara bundled up Marlene, now eight-and-one-half months old, and got ready to leave, never to return again.

One mile west of Elmira Barbara suddenly came up behind a feed truck that was slowing down to turn into a lane. She braked. The road was still slushy from the snow the day before. The car started skidding sideways across the center line, the back end coming around. The oncoming tandem sewage truck hit the car in the driver's door at an angle and tore the two doors and center post out, then hurled the car into the ditch. The truck ended up in the other ditch. Marlene, who had landed on the floor of the passenger side, started crying but Mother did not hear it. Barbara lay quiet and still, very still! The impact on the side of her head killed her instantly.

Barbara's first cousin, Howard Gingrich, was one of the first ones at the scene. The truck driver was not hurt. When he realized that he was instrumental in taking a life into eternity, his question was, "Was she a Christian?" He was concerned. Marlene was taken to the hospital by ambulance. Barbara was taken to the same hospital later.

Levi Brubacher was at B & M Farm Equipment one-fourth mile away when he noticed, "Looks like there's been an accident!" So he drove over. When he walked up to the car, he saw there was still someone in it. Upon seeing her covering, he inquired of others if they know who this is.

After being informed, he asked if someone had gone to bring her parents word. Since he knew Norman and Lovina Brubacher, Barbara's parents, he offered to go. After starting off he thought, "I should have someone to go with me." Almost on impulse he turned in at Elmira Farm Service and asked the bookkeeper, Aaron Diefenbacher, who also knew Normans well, to go with him. They drove the five miles to Normans and broke the news to Barbara's mom. Her dad was cutting wood in the bush on the other farm, so it was decided that Aaron would stay in the house, while Levi goes to the bush to tell Norman. After telling him, they started walking out of the bush together when Norman said, "This chainsaw is getting too heavy to carry!" The shock was starting to work on him, too. Lovina had in mind that Barbara was going to stop in at Melvins in the morning, before coming to their place. Marion had in mind she would stop in on the way home in the evening, so neither of them was getting anxious as the hours passed by without Barbara showing up.

That morning my father, Alvin, had planned to go to a meeting in Guelph. He picked up a neighbor and they were on their way. Eventually they came to the accident and as they were slowly driving past, the neighbor said, "That man wants to stop you!" Howard had recognized my father! It was quite a shock for him to find out that his daughter-in-law was gone.

Meanwhile, in Wroxeter we were unloading the bagged fertilizer off the side of the flat bed trailer onto pallets which we had strung out on the side of the street. Our warehouse was an old church shed where the people had tied their horses years ago, while attending church services across the street. So it had no yard at all, therefore we had to park on the street to unload. The trailer had just left and I was on my way to get the forklift when a police car pulled up. My first impulse was that someone had complained that we were blocking this slightly used street too much. His mission, however, was quite something different! My father was about the only one who knew where I was. Therefore, he could instruct the officer how to find me. Since it was in another police district, they radioed that office to send out an officer to notify me. He walked up to me and asked, "Are you Leonard Martin?" I said, "Yes." Then he said, "Your wife just died in the hospital." The way he said it, I got the impression that he thought she was sick in the hospital and has now died. I leaned against the side of the door. Then I felt the Everlasting Arms around me to hold me up, as I yielded to Him. I do not believe that He could have helped me if I had not learned to trust my Savior beforehand. I said, "She was at home this morning, but something could have happened on the road." He seemed kind of lost then and didn't know what to say. I told him I'd find out, and stepped inside the office and phoned her parents. Meanwhile, the officer drove away. When someone answered at the other end, I asked, "Is Barbara there yet?" It was Aaron who had answered the phone and he responded with, "Didn't you find out what happened yet?" Just then the officer came back in and said, "There was an accident!" Then the truth and reality really started to sink in! He was very helpful and suggested that I will likely want to go home. I said, "I should put this fertilizer inside first." "No, just leave it. Shall I take you home?" I had my truck there, but I didn't trust myself to drive home, as I was trembling all over. As we drove the twelve miles home, I asked the officer, "What do we do now?" "Well, you will want to get the family together." Yes, of course! He followed me in, as I went into the house to change clothes. One of the first things I noticed was the sewing machine, standing idle, where Barbara had been sewing the day before. First I called my mother, who was cleaning for a lady in Listowel, like she sometimes did. I'm afraid I was fairly blunt with the way I told her what had happened. We arranged that the officer would take me the ten miles to Listowel and we would meet in the parking lot. The officer made a few calls to the hospital to arrange for us to come there. When we got to Listowel, I thanked the officer for his kind help, then sat in my mother's car. She was the first one of the family I met. With tears she asked, "Is this the way it must be?" We had a good cry together.

We drove the thirty miles to the hospital and met the personnel as arranged. We walked down a long hall, not even knowing our mission. At a certain door the nurse stopped. She said, "We will ask you to identify the body, since you are the nearest of kin. Are you ready?" "I guess." We went through the door and up four steps. My shoes were so heavy! Those were the hardest steps I ever climbed! There was a stretcher with a body on it, totally covered with a white sheet. The nurse pulled back one corner of the sheet far enough so I could see her face and asked, "Is this your wife?" "Yes," but such a battered and bruised face. She put the sheet back again. We went into the hall again where I met the chaplain, who said, "Trust in God." With resignation I answered, "It is our only hope!" Then the nurse asked if we would like to see Marlene? "Oh, yes, where is she?" "On the fourth floor." We took the elevator to the fourth floor where we met another nurse who took us to Marlene's room. She was sleeping peacefully. She had escaped with only a broken nose and sprained left wrist.

My mother and I then headed to Normans where other family members had gathered. My father-in-law met me at the door with a handshake and tears. No words were spoken. What was there to say? I went around the circle and shook hands with each one. The tears flowed freely. We sat together in silence for a while. My father mentioned that Barbara had started off for her earthly home and went to her eternal home instead.

At a time like this we need the church, neighbors and friends to take over and help plan the funeral. I just sat there in a daze. The day finally did come to an end. It seemed like a long time since we had gotten up in the morning. My sister Elsie went home with me that night. On the way we talked of the vacancy at home and who will help care for Marlene and keep house. How very much I appreciated her offer that she would do it. We came home to a dark and quiet house. We went in and saw everything as it was left in the morning.

The next morning we went to Normans to make more arrangements. Later I went to the hospital to visit Marlene. She was awake when I entered her room and was busy doing something in her crib. When she saw me, she stretched out both arms toward me. I picked her up and we clung to each other. At least we still had each other.

The viewing started at seven o'clock on Friday evening, with many people coming to pay their last respect and to offer comfort and sympathy.

Early the next morning Melvin and Marion became parents. Leon, a healthy boy, was born to them. So Marion could not be with us for the funeral, but at least she had seen her sister yet.

On Saturday Marlene was released from the hospital, so we brought her home. At the viewing that afternoon and evening, some people made the comment that "It's too bad this had to happen." It was hard at the time, but if our desire is to walk close with the Lord then this experience has helped to do it. Therefore, it was for the good. This is an experience I will always treasure, to have felt the presence of God so closely.

On Sunday morning the undertaker got so many requests that he opened the doors early, as many would like to come in on their way to church. Soon after ten o'clock the body was brought to the home where Barbara grew up. Home is the place where the experiences of life are centered, so it seemed appropriate to have the body there because death is also a part of our experiences while on this earth. Many people came for the viewing again that day, including some from other states.

After everyone had left that evening, and those at home there had gone to bed, I spent some time alone with my companion. I laid my hand on hers. It was cold. I would encourage family members to do this, as it helps us to realize that this is only the shell that is left. The person or character that we knew is no longer in it. I knelt beside the casket and poured out my heart to our Heavenly Father who comforteth us in time of grief. It was there I committed her to Him who had allowed her to be a part of my life for two short years. Thus, ended our wedded life.

Monday noon a family service was held at the house. As the casket was then carried down the sidewalk to the waiting hearse, I found myself being carried along on the power of other people's prayer. Marlene's great-aunt stayed with her while we went to the church.

At the churchyard, again many people filed past the casket to pay their last respects. Then the family gathered around and in our hearts we bade farewell to one we loved. I am thankful that I was able to commit her to God the evening before which made the parting now easier to bear.

After the body was lowered into the ground, a hymn sung, and the final committal given, we gathered into the meetinghouse to hear the message from God. While the minister from Pennsylvania was preaching, the next minister whispered to our home minister, "He's preaching all the things I had in mind!" The answer was, "The Bible is thick, there are many things in there." So God gave him a different message to say unto the people. Since Marion could not be there, and also for Marlene's sake, someone copied the sermon so they could also benefit from it.

That evening one of my friends said that I should write a letter to a widower in Pennsylvania who had lost his wife a few months before. And so I did. I did not know the man, but that did not matter. He was of the same faith and I felt that we could relate to each other's experiences. After I wrote to him, I soon had a letter in return, and thus began a friendship which continues on until this day.

Among the visitors that came in the months that followed, one couple stood out to me. They were making their own wedding plans and in my sorrow I couldn't understand why people would continue to marry, only to go through the heartache of parting later.

The family gathering that first summer was a painful experience, a reminder that the circle is broken. While singing that afternoon, an uncle sitting beside me suggested we sing "Sister, thou wast mild and lovely." Needless to say, that brought the tears again. However, time has a way of healing and as one quote says, "In three words I can sum up everything I have learned about life, life goes on."

Now twenty-six years later as we reflect over these happenings, let's consider a few things. At the time of parting, we very much long to be united again in heaven. But Jesus said that in the resurrection they neither marry nor are given in marriage but are as the angels of God in heaven. The bond that there is in family relations is the best way God could show us the close relationship He wants with His children. Even though we have hope by availing ourselves of the atonement He made on the cross, we will let Christ be the judge if we will be worthy to enter heaven. Let's be thankful for close family ties and strive to have the same relation with Christ in our spiritual lives, as He will be the main focus in heaven, even though we may recognize people that we knew while on earth.

—*Leonard Martin*
Listowel, Ontario

Noah J. Gingerich
March 8, 1929 to December 17, 1985 (56 years)

All In His Control
Fannie (Gingerich) Troyer, Wife

On December 14, 1985, late at night Noah and I returned to our Plain City, Ohio home. We had been gone for about one and a half weeks visiting with our oldest son David and family in Missouri; and a daughter Susanna and Harold Friesen and newborn in Texas. We were en-route to bring an elderly lady, who had lived in our home for a while, a truckload of her possessions. She had recently moved to San Antonio, Texas.

Yes, we lacked in sleep, but on Monday evening we had lots to talk about. I believe it was God-ordained time as we talked late in the night until 2:30.

The next morning, Tuesday, December 17, dawned as a crisp, cold morning. Noah and our son Vernon were up early to do the chores: milking cows, feeding, etc. Vernon also had some calves to feed at our son Wayne's, since they'd left for a day or two. At 8:30 the chores were done, except for feeding the cows. Vernon would've liked to do the chores at Wayne's before breakfast, so Noah decided he'd feed the cows. Vernon reminded Dad before he left that the bull was out of his pen.

A short time later, at 8:50, some cars slowed down. Catching my attention, one drove in. The man got out of his vehicle and was looking on the ground. I gasped. There was Noah lying on the ground. As I was heading out to Noah, the man met me and said we must call the squad. More people stopped to help and came with blankets and coats to warm him. As soon as I could, I returned to see what I could do. I rubbed his face, called his name, talked to him, and told him we're getting help. Through labored, raspy breaths he moaned and tried twice to say "Yes." I felt he recognized my voice, but that was the only response I could get.

We couldn't see any cuts or bruises, except a small gash above his one eye. Therefore I assumed he must have had a heart attack. We looked for his hat and glasses, but couldn't find them. I quickly made a few calls. Our daughter Esther and David Miller and a few others came to go with us to the hospital soon after the squad left. A brother-in-law kindly began making calls to inform the rest of the 11 children.

Those at the hospital were ready for us and asked the needed questions. They then escorted us to a room where the doctor broke the news to us that he had passed on, with an apparent massive heart attack. Noah was only 56 years of age. After seeing his body and getting his personal belongings, we left the hospital.

On the way home I asked Vernon what was left for Noah to do when he'd left for Waynes. He said he was going to feed the cows. Immediately I knew he had to cross the cow lot and remembered that we couldn't find his hat or his glasses. I asked, "Vernon, was the bull out?!" He said yes, but he'd reminded Dad before he left. The bull was let out earlier and just hadn't been put back in his pen yet.

Esther and Dave had come to the hospital a bit later than we, since a neighbor had seen the squad and stopped by to see if he could help with the chores or anything.

Esther, having helped with the chores a lot before marriage, checked to see if the feeding was done, and noticed a bucket setting on the cattle guard, which Noah had to cross.

Thus talking about this on the way home, we concluded he was trying to thaw a frozen cattle waterer with hot water. It was located in the corner of the cow lot, just inside the cattle guard.

Dave and Esther had concluded the same and went out immediately on their return home, in search of Noah's glasses and hat, to determine better the cause of death. They found his glasses broken in many pieces inside the waterer and on the other side of the fence. Also his hat lay a short distance away in the cow lot, a bit manured and looking beaten. They also checked for blood on the lane which he crossed to where he had lain in front of the barn. But a light snow had fallen and they couldn't find his path of about 120 feet. He must have walked somehow, since the knees of his coveralls showed no sign of crawling, neither were they wet from the ice and snowy ground.

After Daves, Vernon, and our youngest daughter, Vera, came in with the remains, we concluded that he probably had his back turned to the bull. Being either deep in thought or maybe singing as he often did, he never heard the approach of the bull.

At noon a doctor from the Franklin County Coroner's Office called out to the home and talked with Ora, Noah's brother, and said that their examination of Noah's body have given them evidence that he died of a massive heart attack and that there was no foul play involved in his death. Thereupon Ora stated that we now have evidence that it was otherwise. He at once asked,"What is this? Did you call the police?" and several other questions as if he thought that we meant there was foul play involved in his death. Ora said, "No, there was no foul play in his death, he was crushed to death by a bull." He then asked, "What is a bull?" He told him a bull is a male cow. He then said, "I know what a cow is, but I don't know what a bull is." He then offered to take x-rays of the body for us. Ora heard him ask another doctor about it and then he said he will call back later. He called back about a half-an-hour later and said, "They took x-rays and found that his pelvis was broken and that his abdomen was filled with blood which caused his death. Their findings have determined that Noah was crushed to death by an animal." He also had a belt-like bruise across his lower abdomen, where he'd been pushed against the waterer.

We have reasons to believe Noah suffered much pain for a short while in walking this 120 feet before collapsing out in front of the barn. We were told later that it doesn't take more than 15 minutes for a person to bleed to death internally.

Our home was soon filled with many sympathizers: relatives, friends, and a lady from church was here by noon already with chili soup. Our hearts were richly blessed by the many who lent helping hands so generously and endeavored to comfort to the best of their ability during this shocking time.

The bull was owned by a "company" of five men, and Noah being one of them, was caring for the bull. That evening yet some of the men came to get the bull. He was hauled off and sold to be slaughtered. A few days later we received the check of the proceeds, which the men generously gave to help with the expenses.

Dad was cautious and had built a pen for the bull just prior to the trip, for safety's sake, and probably for a peace of mind. Only God knows and we believe He had things all in His control as they took place that morning.

—Submitted by: Jonas Gingerich, Son
Nappanee, Indiana

Father's Day . . . It's Different Now

I cannot send a gift or card to wish him "Happy Father's
  Day,"
So I'm asking You to tell him Lord, the things I want to say.
Tell him first in gentle tone, how very much we care,
How glad we are to be his own, and long to meet him
  there.
Tell him I'm very grateful for the years together we had,
There's never another just like him, our kind and loving
  dad!
Tell him I miss his wise advice on problems great or small,
But not how my grief at his leaving sometimes overshadows
  all.
Don't mention the lonely hours I listen in vain for his call,
Nor how my heart aches in sadness for him who was "my
  all."
Tell him the children remember the many good things he
  taught,
The kindly way he explained what we should do or should
  not.
Father's Day just isn't the same now that he has gone away,
Tell him, Lord, that I love him, He's with you this Father's
  Day.

-Author Unknown

JOHN R. RAMER, Jr.
April 12, 1954 to May 29, 1991 (37 years)

Underneath Are The Everlasting Arms
Linda E. (Ramer) Martin, Wife

Death can be final, cold, painful, and heart-rending... But think—death is but the gateway to LIFE, heaven, eternal bliss, peace, joy, happiness! No sickness or tears. Surrounded by Jesus' very own presence, the ransomed millions and the heavenly angels, death is not to be feared for those who have sent their sins on before to be taken away by the precious blood of Jesus!

We knew John had cancer for approximately three years before it claimed his life. The first symptoms were swollen glands on his neck. We and the doctors were not alarmed at first, as his glands had occasionally swelled before when he was fighting a cold or other germs. This time the swelling did not recede as it had previously, but as a few months passed, another gland became swollen.

A biopsy was taken which revealed his cancer to be Chronic Lymphocytic Leukemia (CLL). It starts in the lymph glands and moves to the blood, thus the leukemia. CLL is a disease of people over age 60. At age 34, John was the youngest CLL patient the specialist had ever seen. There is no cure for CLL but it can be controlled by medication in older folks. In the rare event that CLL strikes a younger person, it is much more aggressive and harder to treat than when an older person has it.

With CLL the bone marrow produces too many white blood cells. We need white cells to fight infection, so what is wrong with that? When the white blood cell count increases, the red blood cell (RBC) count must decrease. Red blood cells are our energy cells, so the person becomes tired. Also these many white blood cells that the body is making are not properly formed. They are immature and cannot even fight infection.

This condition is treated with micro doses of chemotherapy. The doses are large enough to suppress the WBC count, yet small enough that the patient has no adverse side effects, such as hair loss or nausea. For this we were thankful.

Because of the aggressive nature of John's CLL, he would be off the medication for only a few weeks until he would need to be back on it. While on the medication, he would be extra tired as it also suppressed his red cell count.

For most of those three years, he could work on his job for only three hours a day. Then he was too tired and needed to come home and rest. This put us into a financial crisis. When he was diagnosed, Rhoda was three. Five months later Rachel joined our family. She was a cheerful child and brightened many sad hours for both John and me. Prior to her birth, I wondered why we needed this added responsibility now, but God knew we needed the blessings of our two girls.

John asked to be anointed three months after we were told that he had cancer. We committed his life to God, whether He planned physical healing or a new body. Even though we would have chosen the physical healing, we believe God blessed in other ways instead. John prayed many times that he would be spared from suffering much pain, as a sister in our congregation was suffering a lot of pain from cancer. Our hearts went out to her. Although John had much weariness as a result of his cancer, he was spared from severe pain until the last six hours of his life. Even the undertaker was surprised by this fact. We believe this was a special blessing from God.

John's condition continued fairly stable, with its roller-coaster rides of needing a two-week dose of chemotherapy, then being off of it for a few weeks, then back on. Our hopes would soar as the chemotherapy took effect, then crash as we saw the WBC count once again rising.

In February of 1991 the chemotherapy brought the RBC count and hemoglobin (Hbg) to dangerously low levels. In the following six weeks he received blood transfusions, totaling fifteen units of RBC. Then his blood counts stabilized and he needed no more transfusions for seven weeks. Our hopes soared!

Suddenly John's blood counts plunged lower than they ever were before. This resulted in popping the blood vessels in the back of the retinas of his eyes. His vision was very clouded. At this same time he also started having high fevers. These two factors kept him home from work and in bed all the time.

For two weeks the doctors took various tests with no conclusions. His fevers could no longer be controlled with Extra-Strength Tylenol. The doctor prescribed a pill to take along with the Tylenol. He also started taking radiation treatments for his enlarged spleen. It was so large that he was short of breath from the pressure exerted on his lungs. He could barely eat because of the pressure it put on his stomach.

After returning home from his second radiation treatment, the radiologist called to discontinue the treatments because John's platelet count was down to 7,000; normal is 140,000 to 400,000. A few minutes later the specialist called and made arrangements for John to come to the hospital the next day for two units of red blood cells and ten units of platelets. This was to be the first platelet transfusion. The family doctor also called. His message was the same—doctors could do nothing else for John.

How does a person tell their companion that they are going to die? I heard John coughing so I knew he was awake. I went to check on him, turning over in my mind how to break the news to him. But he brought up the subject when he asked, "Do you think I'm going to make it?" I told him the doctors' opinions that his bone marrow was no longer producing blood cells. His life was in God's hands. He expressed his readiness and longing for heaven, but also his extreme reluctance to leave the girls and me. We cried together at the thought of parting.

We discussed funeral plans, not knowing we would need them the next day. John chose several songs, one having deeply impressed him in the last several months:

"More love to thee, O Christ,
More love to thee,
Hear thou the prayer I make
On bended knee...
Let sorrow do its work,
Send grief and pain;
Sweet are thy messengers,
Sweet their refrain,
When they can sing with me:
More love, O Christ, to thee...
Then shall my latest breath
Whisper thy praise;
This be the parting cry
My heart shall raise;
This still its prayer shall be:
More Love, O Christ, to Thee,
More love to Thee,
More love to Thee."

-Elizabeth P. Prentiss

Next he called Rhoda, then six, to his bedside. When he told her he might pass away soon, she burst out crying. He expressed his concern for her to grow up to learn to love Jesus.

He also requested the ministry to gather that evening for meditation with him. He chose two songs to sing. We opened the service there in our bedroom by singing, "On Jordan's Stormy Banks I Stand." Verse three was very impressive:

> "No chilling winds nor poisonous breath
> Can reach that healthful shore,
> Sickness and sorrow, pain and death
> Are felt and feared no more."
> —Tullius C. O'Kane

The bishop brought our thoughts to several passages on heaven, reading from John 14:1-6, II Corinthians 5:1-4, I Corinthians 15:49-58, and I Thessalonians 4:13-18. We concluded with John's second song selection, "There's A City Of Light."

Following a rough night of fevers, coughing, a swollen lip and bleeding from his mouth, we rose to face his last day on earth. (We did not realize that, of course.) Before we left for the hospital, he had more strange symptoms—his hands shook and his leg jumped uncontrollably. It took two of us to help him the short distance from the house to our deacon's waiting van.

Within an hour of arriving at the hospital, he started having excruciating pain in his legs, and his face continued to swell. When the doctor came, she put him on morphine and began the platelet transfusion. She felt the red blood cells she had planned to give him might only serve to prolong his suffering, so they were not given.

The swelling continued to increase, going up the right side of his face, swelling his eye shut. The doctor thought a rapid-moving infection had set in a small sore inside his lip, causing the swelling.

As the morning progressed, John would lift up his hands occasionally. He kept repeating three phrases: "Open the gates," "Pull me up," and "Lord, take me home." Later I asked him if he saw angels and his answer was an emphatic "Yes!" He gave the same response to the questions, "Do you see heaven?" and "Do you see Jesus?"

Brother Ira Mast, our deacon who was with us, found a Bible in the chapel and John seemed much comforted by what Brother Ira read. He especially liked II Corinthians 5:1-2. *"For we know that if our earthly house of this tabernacle were dissolved, we have a building of God, an house not made with hands, eternal in the heavens. For in this we groan, earnestly desiring to be clothed upon with our house which is from heaven."* I was impressed with Brother Ira's selection of verses. Even though he had been unable to attend the bedside service the evening before, he was reading many of the same verses that had been read then.

Brother Ira asked John if there were any verses that he would like to share. Even though he could hardly speak due to the swelling, he said, *"Trust in the Lord with all thine heart; and lean not unto thine own understanding"* (Proverbs 3:5). This had been one of his favorite verses.

Around 1:45 p.m. Brother Aaron Shank, our bishop, came in and asked John if he's looking forward to going to heaven and seeing Jesus. He could no longer talk because his mouth was too badly swollen, but responded with an emphatic, "AH-HUH!"

Half-an-hour later our minister Brother Clair and wife Verna Burkholder came. His eyes were both swollen shut, so I told him, "Clair and Verna are here to see you." He nodded his head and moaned in response to let me know he had heard. Fifteen minutes later, at 2:30 p.m., John's spirit silently took its flight to the realms above. As he drew his last shallow breath, and through my weeping and tears, brightly flashed the phrase, "Underneath are the everlasting arms." How precious!

His short earthly life was over. But the girls and I needed to go on. Rachel was only two and would never remember her daddy. Rhoda was six and looking forward to starting school in a few months. The day after John died was to be our tenth wedding anniversary. Now funeral plans needed to be made instead of observing anniversaries. Dresses needed to be sewed. I had decided the girls and I would wear black. I never before had a black dress. About three weeks previous, I had bought a piece of black fabric. Two days before John died, on my birthday, I had cut it and stuck it away. So when I couldn't sleep at night, I got up and sewed our dresses.

The text for John's funeral was taken from Deuteronomy 33:27. *"The eternal God is thy refuge, and underneath are the everlasting arms."* I had requested this text, as this is what came to my mind as John drew his last breath. It was as if an audible voice spoke to me. God's presence was very real at that moment. Heaven seemed so close, almost as if I could reach out and touch it. How I longed to go along with my dear one...

For days I basked in the glory of John's last day on earth and the closeness I felt to heaven. But gradually reality set in. Adjustments needed to be made. Decisions faced me. Questions and problems plagued my mind. My appetite was gone. I needed to force every bite down. Soon I weighed only 97 pounds.

Evenings were naturally the worst. They were the times John and I discussed matters and shared concerns. How I missed his companionship! So in the evenings after the girls were in bed, I started filling a note book with poems, Scripture verses, and words of songs that spoke of heaven.

In days of distress and tears, many times I read over these and they were a help and comfort to me. Later I started a journal.

In our bedroom were two wooden mottos with verses painted on them. These verses became very precious to me: *"For with God all things are possible"* (Mark 10:27). *"But my God shall supply all your need according to his riches in glory by Christ Jesus"* (Philippians 4:19).

Needs? Yes, I had plenty! Financially, the church had helped us out very much those years while John was ill and could only work three-hour days. About a year before he died, we opened a small store in our home. Adding some items I had sewed to the selection of boxed cards opened up another door. Soon sewing orders started pouring in and I was kept busy! Now that John was gone, I determined to support myself with the store and my sewing. God did supply for our needs. Many times I was moved to tears at the kindnesses of Christian friends and family members when gifts of food and other tokens of love arrived at my door.

I felt so insufficient to deal with the needs of my grieving daughters. How does one relate to a child who faces the death of a parent when you haven't experienced that yourself? How could I comfort Rhoda the many times when she would wake up in the night screaming, or walk in her sleep? How could I reach out when my heart itself was so heavy with the burden of grief I carried? How could I bear to send my firstborn off to her first day of school without her daddy by her side? John had anticipated this day so much. I Peter 5:7 became precious to me: *"Casting ALL your care upon him; for he careth for YOU."* I paraphrased Psalm 132:1 to read, "Lord, remember *Linda* in all *her* afflictions."

Another great need came into focus exactly three months after John's funeral. There would be a church division. We had felt it coming for quite a while but now the awful truth became official. I felt torn! I knew that those that had helped us so much, who had stood by his dying bedside, who had supported me as I went alone from there—some were going one way—some the other. My sad heart felt pulled to pieces. The implications of my decision were far reaching. I had daughters who needed to be brought up in the ways of truth and right. How was I to know which way would be best for them down the road several years? Finally, after much prayer and many discussions, I committed it to the Lord. Since I had no husband to direct me, I asked the Lord to give me some clear sign to know the way that I should take. I wanted God's best for my girls and myself. I was sincerely seeking and I wanted to be assured of His leading. I felt confident that God would direct. I especially felt the need for this as the church division started to divide families. My family was going one way, and John's family the other way.

Months passed. I continued praying, seeking God's will. Some day's burdens were more than I could bear it seemed. Then a friend would stop in to visit, or I would get a phone call, or a letter in the mail.

One day the mail contained a letter with a Canadian postmark. "Oh, that must be the lady I had sent recipes to," I thought. I hadn't heard from her for quite a while. Maybe she had heard of John's death. Sure enough, it opened with reference to John's death. But as I started reading the second paragraph, the room around me started spinning. I felt faint. This was not the recipe lady! I had read, "Would you consider a second marriage relationship? I am still single and have always appreciated your testimony since we first met at Bible School."

It seemed as if a hundred thoughts were trying to go through my mind at once. But above them all it was as if an audible voice was saying, "Here is your answer. Here is your answer." I had nearly forgotten about Edgar Martin that I had met thirteen years previously. I was still writing to his sister and so he had kept tabs on my life and had not forgotten me. And God had not forgotten me either. No, the letter before me did not contain the answer to my church dilemma but I felt it would be forthcoming. Our first phone call gave me my answer. God is faithful. He will remember His own!

Not long before our wedding day, I remarked to a close friend that she had helped me through my grief more than anyone else. She looked surprised and wondered how that could be. She had never faced the death of a family member. What had she done that had helped me so much? "Lucy," I said, "When I shared my grieving with you, you didn't criticize me. Instead, you quietly pondered for a while and then you said, 'If I'd be going through what you are going through, I'd probably feel the same way.' And that gave me the courage to pick up and go on. You assured me that my feelings were normal for one who was grieving."

Another friend came to visit one day and asked how it was going. Maybe I shared too much of my deep, dark valley with her. She went to John's cousin and told her that she thinks that I'm taking it too hard and should lean on the Lord more. And that was probably correct. Cousin's answer to her meant a lot to me. She said, "You haven't been through what she is going through. Maybe if you were where she is, it would look different."

After a companion's death, it seems most of us dread the thought of the next funeral we will need to attend. At least I sure did! I needed to face that one month after John's death. John's cousin's son drowned at age eleven. How my grieving, sorrowful heart went out to Jordan's family. Part of me did NOT want to go to that funeral, yet I felt I must reach out to them—they had reached out to me just one month before.

On the way to the funeral I was told that following Jordan's death, his parents found a notebook. In it Jordan was attempting to write me a letter of sympathy. He had made five attempts and also copied a very long poem from the book, "Footprints In The Sand." (This book is available from Pathway Publishers.) The last line of this poem on death is *"God be praised, it is fulfilled."* Jordan had written these words in very large letters. The remarkable thing about this was that Jordan had a crippling form of arthritis and he avoided writing if at all possible. And he had written this for ME! At eleven years old! Had he somehow realized that he would soon be joining John in heaven? This incidence was very touching to me.

Jordan's funeral was a very emotional service because John's death and Jordan's sympathy letters were referred to in the sermon. The poem he had copied for me was also read. It was so fitting. As I walked past Jordan's mother on my way to the grave side, I touched her shoulder. I remember how she cried when I did that. I cried too.

Till I got back home that day, I had a terrible headache and felt sick. That evening a friend stopped in and told me she has news but I must sit down to hear it. A young man I knew had died suddenly of a heart attack, leaving a widow and five fatherless children. That was almost more than I could take.

Even though I have remarried, I will not forget the grief of widowhood—the pain of parting—the lonely hours—the heavy load of responsibility. My heart still grieves deeply each time I hear of a new widow or widower. I feel their pain and pray for them. *"Leave thy fatherless children, I will preserve them alive; and let thy widows trust in me"* (Jeremiah 49:11).

Out of my grief poured forth several poems. Following are two of them:

My Companion

Oh, dear God, my heart is bleeding,
*   It is broken, torn in two,*
For the one who walked beside me
*   Has now gone to be with You.*

I rejoice he's in Your presence,
*   But I miss him by my side.*
As the lonely hours stretch onward,
*   I so many times have cried.*

For ten years we walked together
*   On our journey here below,*
But now from my side he's missing,
*   And now I alone must go.*

So alone I travel onward;
*   Yet alone I never walk,*
I have One who is my Comfort
*   To whom I can always talk.*

And I read His Word and ponder
*   How for widows He does care;*
And I feel His presence near me
*   As I come to Him in prayer.*

Oh, the strength He then does give me
*   For to face this lonely way,*
And prepare to meet my Savior,
*   And my husband some sweet day.*

Oh, the glory he's enjoying!
  Oh, the beauty that is there!
For he now is with his Jesus,
  And he's free from earthly care.

Lord, now help me to be faithful
  In the trials that I meet;
Be my Strength, Companion, Comfort
  'Til I sit at Jesus' feet.

  -Linda, June '91

My Heart Cry

O God, I'm so homesick for heaven;
  My heart, it just cries and it cries,
For the one who has walked here beside me
  Has gone there to be by Your side.

My loneliness now overwhelms me;
  The sorrows and grief are so great;
The burdens are pressing upon me;
  For heaven I can hardly wait.

It doesn't seem fair when I ponder
  How free from all care he must be,
While here I must labor and toil,
  And wait for when You call for me.

Lord, help me to feel right here near me
  Your presence, Your peace, and Your care.
Give strength for the road I am facing,
  And guide me each step, is my prayer.

My future looks dark and it's dreary;
    No light on my path can I see;
But take Thou my hand and just guide me
    To where You would have me to be.

Help me to submit to You daily,
    Help me to rejoice in Your care;
And help me to feel You right here
    To help me my burdens to bear.

                      -Linda, July 1991

                —Linda (Ramer) Martin
                Clinton, Ontario, Canada

"Whilst we are at home in the body, we are absent from the Lord...and willing rather to be absent from the body, and to be present with the Lord" (II Corinthians 5:6, 8).

DANIEL JAMES STEINER
August 7, 1977 to August 29, 1998 (21 years)

Our Disappointment—God's Appointment
Marion Steiner, Wife

I stood on the shore watching the canoe bearing my husband, Daniel (21), and my brother Benjamin (16). Down the lake inlet they went, loaded with supplies for the Devenys. Suddenly the thought came to me, "What if this would be the last time I would see my dear husband?" I took one last look, and turning, I ran up the hill to the van where the rest of the family waited for me.

My seven brothers and sisters, my parents, and Daniel and I, had come three-and-one-half hours north to visit the Devenys. The day was Saturday, August 29, 1998.

Coming to the west end of Munro Lake (Devenys lived close by that lake), we found one of their canoes at the canoe landing. Thinking they had left it there for us, we loaded it with supplies for the Devenys. From there the supplies could be transported by water instead of we carrying them one-half mile through the bush at the end of the road.

Exactly eleven weeks before, Daniel and I had been joined in marriage and we were enjoying the blessings of married life. We, along with my family, had learned to know the Deveny family by a contact we had with them through school and had struck up a friendship.

As we drove to the landing where the footpath to Deveny's house was, an uneasy feeling gripped me. I prayed for Daniel and Benjamin asking God to protect them. Upon our arrival at the footpath I started running toward the house. My sister Esther joined me and we ran the half mile together through the bush. I was the first to reach the house. Michael and Theresa Deveny came out to meet us. I informed them that Daniel and Benjamin were coming in the canoe. A look of horror crossed Theresa's face. Turning around she told her husband what I had said. The same look of horror crossed his face. He said, "I'm going down to meet them." We all ran down to the dock and just as we arrived the canoe pulled up. What a relief! All was well. (Later we found out that particular canoe was the most tipsy canoe. They only trusted the most experienced persons with it and had left it at the canoe landing for their son who was soon coming home. Michael knew all about canoes because he built them.)

We spent an enjoyable morning and afternoon. While the women busied themselves with dinner preparation and also cleanup, the men visited in the living room, covering a number of spiritual topics. Daniel enjoyed such challenging discussions.

Around 4:00 p.m. Daniel came to me wondering if I knew when we would leave for home. He remarked that he'd enjoy going for another canoe ride since he had enjoyed the first one so much. "Would you like to go along?" he asked. I had a fear of water and seeing my hesitation he quickly assured me I didn't need to. "The boys will probably enjoy going along." (The boys were my brothers, sixteen-year-old Benjamin and thirteen-year-old Jonathan.)

The adults prepared to look at slides in the afternoon that my dad had taken in South America. Daniel and the boys got ready to go for a canoe ride. Michael went out to make sure they would take the sturdiest of the canoes and gave them a few instructions. Going to the door with Daniel, he and I said, "Good-by," (never once thinking that it may be our last good-by). I went out to the deck, where I could watch them leave. My last mental picture of him: Daniel was standing by the paddles trying each one while deciding which one he wanted to use. That picture of health and strength was indelibly stamped upon my mind.

After they left, I went back inside to watch them from the bay window overlooking the water. I felt a wee bit uneasy. I tried to push that feeling aside, telling myself that there's probably no need to worry. After a little I saw them turning around to come back to the house. I decided to go out to the dock to meet them, then maybe Daniel and I could go out for a short ride.

When I got out there, I couldn't see them anywhere; so I decided to just wait awhile. Suddenly, I heard a call. The generator was on to run the slide projector, so I couldn't hear the call clearly. My first thought was that perhaps it was a moose call. I ran back up to the house feeling uneasy again. Going into the house I pointed while telling them, "I heard something in that direction." The dogs were barking and howling eerily. Theresa went to the door and told them to be quiet. They obeyed, but she felt awful later, and said she'll never do that again. We realized later that they were probably hearing the boys' call for help. Michael's oldest daughter, Hillary (19), came out and jumped into a canoe and started paddling in the opposite direction of which I had said. She had misunderstood me!

I felt very uneasy by this time. I couldn't stay in one spot. I was on my way back to the house when I heard my name being called. I whirled around and saw a man dressed in black come stumbling toward me. For some reason my first thought was that he was a soldier. I started running and he called again, this time frantically, "Marion, we need help. We've capsized!" Now I recognized him. It was not a soldier at all. It was Benjamin, and he was soaking wet. I sped the rest of the way to the house and shouted the news! Everyone sprang into action. Theresa and Michael jumped into a canoe asking, "Where? Where?" Benjamin pointed. They were off!

The rest of us paced. Finally Dad exclaimed, "I can't stay here. I have to do something! Benjamin, show us where it is." A string of people left for the place where Benjamin had swam to shore: Dad, my sisters Esther, Eva and Tina, and Deveny's youngest daughter Tally, with Benjamin in the lead. I was filled with unexplainable dread and agony. Mom and I paced the deck all the while, praying desperately in our hearts. Suddenly, I saw Michael dive off the canoe into the water. My heart froze. I knew then that someone was either missing or struggling.

Finally, Mom and I gathered the crying little ones, Naomi (4) and Dorcas (2), together in the house and knelt by the sofa. We uttered our pleas for protection to our All-Knowing Father. We wanted the Lord's will, but what if..?

About ten minutes later, we went back outside where we saw a solemn procession coming toward the house—Dad in the lead.

Dad stumbled the last few steps. "Marion," his voice broke, "Daniel's gone —we can't find him!" For a moment all was black and my knees felt as thought they would give way. Dad reached out to steady me. "No!" was my first response. At that moment an unexplainable peace and strength filled my being. The next thing I knew, Hillary came up from the dock. She was all soaked and embraced me while saying over and over, "I'm so sorry! I'm so sorry! I tried finding him, but I couldn't." Later I found out that her mother, who was still in a canoe, had sent her to the house because she feared for Hillary's life. She was an exceptionally good swimmer, but was now extremely cold and wet from repeatedly diving. Even though it was August the water was cold, especially in the deep places.

In a short time Michael and Theresa also came up from the shore offering their sympathies. Dad thought we should notify the police rescue team and others. Since Devenys didn't have a phone, we needed to drive approximately one-half hour to a logging camp. I wanted to go along. I felt like I should be the one to notify Daniel's parents.

In my heart I thought Daniel was probably hanging onto some branches farther down the shore. He couldn't be gone, could he? Dad assured me he had run all along the shore looking and calling.

Later I found out that when Michael and Theresa had gotten to the capsized canoe, Jonathan (13) was still in the water and Daniel had just gone down. Jonathan showed them where he went down. Michael dove into the water repeatedly looking for Daniel. But he couldn't go deep enough and it was quite dark near the bottom.

Needless to say, it was an agonizing ride to the logging camp and back again. At the camp I called Daniel's parents, James and Anne Steiner. Daniel's Dad told me they would come as soon as they could pack. I was so relieved to know they were coming.

While we waited for Michael to make arrangements with the RCMP, Dad and I paced the floors—our hearts heavy with an inexplicable weight. Finally Dad motioned me to come with him into a separate room, where we knelt on the floor imploring God for His strength to hold us up and for wisdom and comfort. I felt a measure of peace after that.

Once the realization that I was a widow hit me, my whole being wrenched at the thought and I broke into sobs. Surely this was just a bad dream and soon everything would be all right! I thought probably once we got back to Devenys' house we would hear they had found Daniel. I badly wanted to go home. I'm not sure why I didn't want to stay there to be with Daniel. Looking back now, I think that the Lord knew I couldn't handle being there when they brought him up from the lake-bottom.

The RCMP (Royal Canadian Mounted Police) diving team was called and they said they would come out the next day since it was too late in the day and it would be dark by the time they would get there. Dad had also called the home ministry. They put the shocking news onto the hotline for the Vanderhoof congregation, which was our home church.

Back at Devenys, Theresa and I stayed in the van while Dad and Michael went into the house, by the footpath to get the rest of our family. What a tearful parting, but what else could be done?

As we headed for home down the dirt road, Jonathan and Benjamin explained what had taken place. They had been on their way back to the dock when Daniel remarked, "Let's go down there a little ways, then we'll go back. It looks so quiet and peaceful down there." They turned into a narrower part of the lake, which was why I hadn't been able to see them when I went down to the dock. They rowed a little ways when Daniel said, "Let's stop for a little and just look at the beauty around us." A few moments passed in peaceful conversation when Daniel suggested that maybe they should head back to the house. They reached for their paddles and started rowing when their "stable" canoe capsized. Remembering Michael's earlier instructions to just stay with the boat, they tried to right it again and again by pulling on the sides, but all to no avail. It just kept flipping. It seemed Daniel had sensed danger when they flipped. He prayed, "Oh, God. Help us in this hour!" They called for help, which was what I heard when I thought it was a moose call. Finally they decided to start for the shore 100 yards away. At first Daniel was ahead but then soon lagged behind. We realized later that he had gotten a gash on the back of his head causing his strength to fail. He was an unusually good swimmer. Benjamin reached the shore first and started running for help. He could see Daniel was struggling. As he left, Daniel called out to him, "Please pray for us!" At this point Jonathan was behind Daniel in the water. Daniel reached back and pulled Jonathan alongside of himself and hung on for a second, but instantly they both began to sink. Unlike a drowning person, he immediately let go, giving Jonathan a gentle push toward the shore. "I'm dying," he told Jonathan and soon went down. After Benjamin swam to shore, he had to master another one-fourth mile over very rugged terrain before reaching Devenys' house.

I cannot explain why, but after I heard Jonathan and Benjamin's account, it gave me a sense of peace knowing that he wasn't struggling somewhere. Daniel was safe in the arms of Jesus. It was his earthly body we were leaving behind. Looking back, I know I was in shock.

We were down the road about one-half hour when we met a police officer who was on his way to investigate the apparent drowning. We stopped. Dad and the boys got out of the van to give some details for the legal documents. Oh, the seat beside me where Daniel had sat that morning was so-o-o empty. Was it only that morning he sat beside me on the van seat?

As we waited, a van loaded with people from our home church at Vanderhoof pulled up in front of us. Upon getting word, they had immediately packed bedding, clothing, etc., and drove the normal three-hour trip in record time. (Before the police officer left, he expressed his amazement at the amount of immediate support we received.) Upon seeing the van, our first reaction was, "No, we don't want to talk to anyone!" But as our dear church family came toward us we knew we needed them. It was a sad, tearful meeting to be sure. Two vans and one pick-up truck had come. After a time of weeping and sharing right there on the road, our minister Brother Jerry Wadel suggested we bow for prayer. It was a sad evening, but I couldn't understand why people didn't realize how happy Daniel was now. I was sure he was singing with the angels. He always loved singing. Later I realized that the Lord's arms were holding me up and mercifully allowing me to be in shock.

After prayer, it was decided several people of our group would go back to stay with Devenys until Daniel's body was found. I was relieved to have someone go there just in case... The rest of us all rode the remaining three hours to Vanderhoof. The ride home along that dirt road was never as dark and as long as that evening.

Two miles from my parents' home, we stopped at Daniel's and my house where Mom went in with me while I collected a few items for the night, and Dad took the rest of the family home. Every turn I made in "our" house, there was another memory of Daniel. Memories rushed at me from every side! Finally, I fell on my knees at *our* bedside while crying out to God in anguish, "Why? Why?" Finally, having collected a few things, Mom and I went to my parents' place with *our* car.

Daniel's body was found by the RCMP diving team the next day, 27 hours later. God was merciful in answering our prayers. Daniel's face was without a visible mark, looking as natural as if he was sleeping.

The following days were extremely draining physically and emotionally. Daniel's family arrived a day later, Sunday evening, following a 30-hour drive. What a tearful meeting, but we were so relieved to be together. We needed each other. One of the things we found taxing was all the legal involvements. Those legal details seemed so harsh and cold.

Humanly speaking, there did not seem to be any logical reason for the canoe to tip, but I like to think of it as the

Lord's loving hand coming down to take one of His children Home.

After the funeral I went with my parents to Barwick, Ontario, Daniel's home congregation, for a memorial service. I then stayed with Daniel's family for two-and-one-half months which was a great blessing to all of us.

One-and-one-half years later, my heart is filled with gratitude for the Lord's graciousness in bringing me through each lonely hour and leading me through each dark valley. I do not know what I would have done without both of our families, and the church family; they were a tremendous support. There were times when the road ahead looked impossible, but it was then that the Lord carried me.

In May of 1999, Michael Deveny erected a wooden monument, in memory of Daniel, at Munro Lake. It bears Daniel's name, date of birth, and date of death. We appreciate this act of kindness.

We long for the day when we shall meet our loved one in the air.

—Marion Steiner
Vanderhoof, British Columbia, Canada

"Precious in the sight of the Lord is the death of his saints" (Psalm 116:15).

GLEN S. BURKHOLDER
JUNE 25, 1943 to JULY 14, 1982 (39 years)

———❧❧———

LARRY M. BURKHOLDER
OCTOBER 28, 1969 to JULY 14, 1982 (12 years)

———❧❧———

Small Airplane Tragedy
Irene Burkholder, Wife & Mother

With the help of God I will try to write about the tragedy of my dear husband, Glen (39) and son, Larry (12). Also in the crash were Glen's cousin Willis Burkholder (44) who was the pilot and Willis' son, Charles Burkholder (17).

Glen and Larry left home about 3:00 a.m. and met Willis and Charles at Lancaster Airport. They had planned a day's ground hog hunting trip in New York. (This was not Willis and Glen's first trip to New York.) So on Wednesday, July 14, 1982, they decided this time to each take their only sons along for the day. They left Andover Airport in New York around 9:00 p.m. to return home.

Willis was known to be a safe pilot, and always had prayer before leaving on a flight. Soon after takeoff they heard of storm warnings in the area. The storm brought them out of control and the plane crashed into one of the highest mountain peaks of Potter County, Pennsylvania.

My daughters, Glenda (16), Karen (8), Sandra (7), and I were awaiting their return home. I was sleeping and awakened, thinking something happened. But no, I didn't want to think that so I tried to sleep again.

Glen and Larry had thought they would return home around midnight. I was awakened again around 1:00 a.m. and then called Willis' wife, Ruth. She said they were taking Charles to Bible school at Chambersburg, so they would be running late. So we waited until about 4:00 or 5:00 o'clock in the morning. I called Ruth again and she said she would call the Federal Aviation Administration. She returned the call and said they will start a search. They searched all day Thursday and thought they spotted a plane at nightfall.

Friday they searched again, and by noon we got reports that they all were killed instantly. Two Fathers and their only sons—what a tragedy!

We lived on a hog and steer farm. When I look back, I wonder how we ever came through something like this. But the Lord was at our side and we felt the prayers of the people. What would we do without good Christian neighbors, family, and friends?

We had a 150-sow, farrow-to-finish operation, plus 120 steers at the home farm. Our daughters and I worked together one day at a time...

Now the oldest daughter and her family are farming on the home farm. Our other two daughters live close by and we all work together. I have seven granddaughters and two grandsons, and get the privilege of helping babysit. As I look back, I realize all the prayers of the people helped us through this trial. When you need help, the Lord is ready at all times to help each and every new day.

The Lord has blessed us in many ways. God's grace is sufficient!

—Irene Burkholder
Stevens, Pennsylvania

CARL S. MARTIN
January 17, 1956 to January 12, 1994 (37 years)

Hitherto Hath The Lord Helped Us
Irene M. Martin, Wife

Carl was diagnosed with lupus in February of 1986 at age 30 years. There were several hospital visits throughout the years until 1993. Usually his health was good enough to live pretty much a normal life. Although we knew this sickness had no cure, but that it was somewhat controllable, I still hoped Carl would be able to be here to help raise our family of eight children. If I would start imagining about him dying, I would stop myself and think of others who had lupus for a long time and were still alive. So just because Carl had lupus didn't mean he was going to die soon. Since lupus is not a cancer and is less predictable than some cancers, there was no time limit set for length of life.

March of 1993 was the first of seven hospital visits that year. Carl's stomach wasn't functioning properly but was given help and relief while in the hospital.

April saw Carl back in the hospital again for a few days for fluid retention. It was then decided to do a round of chemotherapy once a month for six months because of failing kidneys. The first dose was too strong so it killed off too many good cells which resulted in infection that needed isolation in the hospital which was the third visit that year. That was in the month of May. During that stay a PIC

(Peripheral Intravenous Catheter) line was inserted and I was taught how to administer the medications.

But by July 7, this PIC line had become infected so Carl needed to be hospitalized a fourth time when the PIC line was removed and he was given antibiotics. (Carl was one that liked to leave the hospital as soon as possible so he was pleased when he was allowed to go home a few days earlier than the doctor had first stated.) All that time fluid kept building up in his body until the beginning of August when he finally consented to go on dialysis and also surgically put a graft in his arm for future use in future dialysis.

Between 50 and 60 pounds of fluid were taken off in a week's time. After that hospital visit Carl's schedule for dialysis at the clinic was Tuesday, Thursday, and Saturday. It took us 45 to 60 minutes to drive the distance. I did not go along for his first dialysis at the clinic. People from church offered to take him sometimes, which freed me to do more things at home. I would have liked to be with him more at times but the children needed me, too. The Lord gave extra ability to stand the strain of these days.

By the end of August the graft that had been put into Carl's arm for use in dialysis had become infected. So we went back to the hospital the sixth time to have the graft removed. Also he was started on total nutrition I-V which was hooked up to the vascular catheter that was used for dialysis. He hardly had an appetite so the I-V fed him and he didn't need to eat much.

After that hospital stay there were various doctor visits and the dialysis schedule to keep up with through September, October, and November.

The night of December 8, 1993 Carl was feeling worse again and by morning he had severe abdominal pain. It was time to be dialyzed again so the doctor said to go ahead as usual with dialysis and then get checked out.

That afternoon Carl was admitted to the hospital for the seventh and last time in 1993. After the doctors consulted together on what to do, it was decided to do a laparotomy (exploratory surgery) that night yet. The main thing that was found was peritonitis which could not be helped surgically but with medicine. Also they thought they found vaculitis, but later dropped that idea.

Through those five weeks of hospitalization Carl was in the ICU four different times and received between 30 and 40 units of red cells plus other blood parts.

Finally after four weeks a doctor talked to us privately to say what I had hoped wouldn't be. Carl would not go home again! (Carl had wanted to go home to be with his Lord but didn't feel right about that desire. After thinking about it he said he was willing to stay for my sake.) Now when I said to him, "I guess I won't have you long anymore," his response was, "You don't know." Perhaps he didn't realize how low he actually was physically.

It was sometime during that last year that I came across these words: *"Do not pray for easy lives, pray to be stronger men! Do not ask for tasks equal to your powers, ask for powers equal to your tasks!"* -Philip Brooks. Those words were an inspiration to me. Surely we would be given strength to experience what the Lord had for us.

The Saturday before Carl's death on Wednesday the three oldest children came in the evening to visit. I took the opportunity to tell them that their daddy was going to die. The oldest daughter (14) responded with, "No, it can't be!" I told the oldest son (16) that he will need to help me and he bravely and gravely agreed to do this. The third one (13), a son, quietly shed some tears. To have broken this news to them gave me somewhat of a relieved feeling.

The next day the fourth child (11), also a son, came to visit. (The children were staying at different homes.) When I told him what I had told the others he wondered if we couldn't pray for Daddy's healing. So he and I went into a little sitting room and knelt and prayed for Daddy's healing, remembering to pray for God's will to be done. Of course many prayers were ascending on our behalf.

The next two daughters, (8) and (9), came later in the day and I also told them the sad news, but there wasn't much reaction on their part. I didn't talk to the three and five-year-old about it. I didn't see them very often. Carl said good-by to the six oldest and gave them admonitions.

The last time Carl was dialyzed the blood wanted to foam which hindered the dialyzing and also told the doctor what condition Carl's liver was in—his liver was failing. When that last dialysis was done it was discovered that Carl's abdominal incision had opened up three to four inches even though it was one month since surgery.

The next morning, Monday The nephrologist came and told me, "You know I fight as long as I can, but to keep on trying to dialyze would just prolong the inevitable." I needed to sign a consent allowing them to discontinue dialysis which of course would bring death. When I told Carl what the doctor wanted and that I consented, I asked him if I did the right thing. His answer was, "I am resigned to it."

The lupus doctor was also there that morning and wanted to tell me that something went wrong with Carl's liver and he didn't know what caused it.

This same doctor talked with me and helped me consent to giving the authority that Code Blue should not be used on Carl—all this in preparation for his death!

The last few days we sang songs of heaven around Carl's bed there in the hospital. He especially liked, "How Beautiful Heaven Must Be." It was hard to imagine that I was able to sing at the time of waiting for death to come, but instead it seemed to help the waiting. God does supply the grace that is needed in each of our experiences. After the funeral the ability to sing those songs without crying was not mine. Or just even the thought of them made me cry.

The thoughtfulness of the nurses and doctors was much appreciated. It was very helpful too to have family and friends around us so much of the time, especially at the last.

Through it all I wanted our lives to be a witness for our Lord. Did our light shine enough those five weeks in the hospital? One nurse expressed herself after hearing us singing that Carl's experience had made her have more faith in God and in family.

It was thought Carl would bleed to death that Sunday night his incision opened up, but he didn't. Monday night the doctor thought Carl might not make it through the night, but he did. Tuesday afternoon a nurse thought that evening would bring the last, but it didn't. Only God knew when Carl would take those last breaths. After such irregular breathing, the last breath came at 12:45 a.m. Wednesday, January 12, 1994.

We wonder, did he see Jesus before he died when he said his last understandable word, "Jesus." (He was on morphine so it was hard to rouse him at the last.)

Oh, the memories! But God has made it possible to bear. Truly He does give strength to the weak when He allows hard experiences to come the way. I was told by my aunt, who had also lost her husband, that God doesn't give us the whole amount of grief at one time but only gives as much as we can bear at a time. That proved to be true.

The grief and sorrow felt as if one would be pinned down so that moving the muscles could not help the least bit to free one's self. Also I felt at first like I was held out in open space just dangling there, no place to get a hold of, no way of helping myself. Most of the first year I so often felt like I was keeping my nose just above the water.

Grief is something you can't shake off. One cannot run away from it—we need to go *through* it. A person has to stop trying to get away from it and just give up and let God give the strength... submission...

We need to desire to grow spiritually through this experience which God is ever delighted to help us do. I like the scripture that says, *"Hitherto hath the Lord helped us."* Not all has been easy but our physical needs are more than amply met. And God's grace is abundant for the rest.

I found it helpful to read about grief. Also there were certain poems that seemed to express my feelings which I recorded in a notebook which I had for that purpose. When reading books or articles and I would come across a certain part that helped me or I wanted to remember, I would write it in that notebook. Sharing with other widows has also been a source of inspiration.

Because Carl was needing another watch, I had bought one for him shortly before he went to the hospital the last time. The thought came to me that Carl's "time" has ended, but time keeps moving on. The watch has kept running and running which helps me see that time didn't stop when Carl died even though some things seem to have come to a "standstill."

We saw the "time" moving on when there needed to be another ordination for minister to fill the place that Carl had filled for eleven years. I didn't like the thought of someone else taking that place. Someone made the comment that no one could take his place but the position needed to be filled. Even so, the ordination was a time somewhat like burying Carl all over again—a strong reminder of his absence.

As the children grow older we see another reminder that time does not stop when a dear one passes on. The children did not bring up the subject about their daddy as much as I did at the beginning, but I think as time is moving on more memories are being spoken of.

There are struggles to face, but God is faithful and has promised, *"But my God shall supply all your need according* to *His riches in glory by Christ Jesus"* (Philippians 4:19). We need to claim these precious promises by faith and *"press toward the mark."*

—*Irene M. Martin*
Anna, Illinois

"Let not your heart be troubled: ye believe in God, believe also in me." "I will come again, and receive you unto myself; that where I am, there ye may be also." "Peace I leave with you, my peace I give unto you: not as the world giveth, give I unto you. Let not your heart be troubled, neither let it be afraid" (John 14:1, 3, 27).

JOHN RAMER
September 9, 1955 to December 31, 1998 (43 years)

Precious Memories - Lonely Hours
Rachel Ramer, Wife

January 1984 when son Orvie was three weeks old, John fainted in the barn while leading our stallion to the water trough for a drink. He was a healthy young man at 29 years old. The next three weeks he was very weak and lay on the couch with flu-like symptoms. The doctors said that the corpuscles in his blood were unbalanced causing them to suspect leukemia. That was ruled out, so they supposed he only had the flu. But he hadn't been ill until he fainted.

(Thirteen-and-one-half years later he was diagnosed with a cancerous brain tumor. Then the doctors suggested that possibly a slow-growing benign tumor had started growing, and was pressing on a nerve when he had fainted.)

Time went on. John was never free from battling health problems after the diagnosis was made, but he had resolved to not let people know how he felt. Who would want to be an ailing person or have others show pity? Not John...

Several years later, after seeing many different doctors and undergoing many tests, the doctors finally suggested stomach ulcers. John was often bloated, his neck and shoulder muscles ached after eating. All these years he could not tolerate water. He was on a strict ulcer diet for two years, with no satisfactory result. Packing lunch for a working man on an ulcer diet was really a challenge. John put in long hours with a carpenter crew. When he came home, he worked on our dairy farm till late at night. He was often tired. There was lots of worry and stress in his life, which can be a factor in causing cancer.

By this time we were the parents of six healthy children. John had quit his carpenter job, and worked at home most of the time, taking on a few remodeling jobs now and then. He also tinkered in his wood working shop, making various small items including clocks and knife holders. John also enjoyed building several kitchen cabinets for neighbors and friends. Oh, the precious memories of these years when the children and I were out with Dad as much as possible. John taught me to do many things around the farm, from driving a six-horse team for harrowing, milking cows, and changing thermostats in the greenhouse, to using skill saws and other tools in the shop.

We always did love to work together. It was nothing unusual for us to come in for a meal, and John would pick up toys and sweep the floor while I prepared the meal. John often put the children's boots and coats on them after meals. He took the children along out whenever he was working so I could come out sooner. We sawed wood and fixed fences, or whatever there was to do. Seldom a day went by that I didn't think of thanking our Maker for a husband to walk by my side. I think I was especially conscious of that as I had two brothers who heard their calling at a young age, leaving widows and children to tarry on.

In 1979 my brother Daniel Imhoff died at age 35 years, leaving a family of young children and his wife, Pauline. Oh, the pain of parting.

In 1981 my mother died leaving my father so lonely. He remarried in 1983.

In 1986 my brother Heber died at 34 years leaving six children and his wife, Hettie. An infant preceded him in death. Hettie was blessed with a baby girl in 1987, after Heber's death.

So I felt I had many reasons to be thankful for my wonderful partner. All these years we knew that not all was well. We searched out one doctor after the next. John had complete physicals, blood work, and all kinds of tests. We saw many chiropractors, too. But no doctor had thought of doing an MRI of John's head. Had we known what we learned through all the hospitals and surgeries, we would have insisted on an MRI much earlier.

In the fall of 1995 we were blessed with another daughter. We now had eight healthy children. That winter John's left foot began to drag. After seeing many professionals, he was diagnosed with sciatic nerve problems, which really had nothing to do with it. With time that problem improved slightly.

That winter John's earthly Father was carried to his grave. That was a hard shock. We found him dead out in the snow between his house and ours when we returned home from an afternoon of running errands. How we hoped death had been instant. John's mother had died in 1989.

The year of 1996 brought no drastic changes. Over the years it was nothing new for John to toss and turn with sore muscles in the back of his neck and shoulders, causing sleepless nights. We tried various things while trying to find relief.

In the spring of 1997, John experienced more trouble. It just seemed like his left arm and hand no longer obeyed his brain's commands. Then on Good Friday morning as John was leading a colt, due to his slow reactions, his arm was badly broken between the colt and a post. The arm healed very slowly and never did regain its original strength. The tumor was on the right side of his brain, and was already affecting the blood flow on his left side—unknown to us.

As summer progressed, John found difficulty in keeping his balance and started drifting toward the left. He never wanted to complain much. One day while baling straw at a neighbors, he lost his balance twice and fell off a wagon. The following Sunday John lost his balance when putting his hat on a hook in church, nearly falling. Also, it took much effort for him to sit upright.

Monday the doctor treated him for ear infection. John's condition was worsening fast. By Wednesday we insisted on an MRI. So to the hospital we went in the afternoon. John drove the horse as we journeyed to the hospital in a very prayerful atmosphere.

The doctors wanted to keep him in the hospital. The MRI showed a large brain tumor. We begged the doctors to let us go home, tell the family, then have a neighbor take us back to the hospital. It was a very hard trip home. Many tears were shed and prayers were sent heavenward as we traveled the 12 miles homeward. It was also very hard to break the news to the children. The oldest of our eight children was 19 years old, and the youngest four days near two years.

August 15 (my forty-third birthday) John was in surgery for three hours. The doctors spent the first two-and-one-half hours getting to the brain tumor and one-half hour closing up again. While he was still asleep in intensive care, I left our friends and family at the hospital and went home to break the news. That was an almost unbearable task, to reveal the diagnosis to my children. One son was missing—out delivering produce. My heart ached as we were not all together already. Yes, Dad's brain tumor was cancerous. There was no hope. It was very fast growing. John's life expectancy was from three to six months. Oh, precious minutes... Never again did I want to leave his side.

August 23, we were home again from the hospital. John had six weeks of radiation therapy, which doctors hoped would slow down the tumor growth. Oh, how our hopes rose and we prayed for a miracle when at the end of the radiation, the MRI showed the tumor was gone! Nothing remained but scar tissue. Since this was a recurring glioblastoma multiform tumor, the doctors expected the tumor to return.

John had follow-up MRI's monthly. We searched nationwide for help for our much-needed daddy. My human mind thought, "My ways, my child, are not your ways." We sent many test results to various doctors and clinics till we learned of a very talented doctor in Florida.

This brain surgeon had much experience. We found that he also used treatments called Gamma Knife on brain tumors. (There are now four clinics like his in the United States. At that time there were only two.) Since John could have no more radiation, we decided on a trip to Florida.

By this time John had regained strength and appeared much like a healthy man, other than the loss of hair on the right side of his head. His color was better than it had been for years. The trip to Florida was for prevention and to try slowing down recurring cells. The doctor there told us on our first consultation that he could not cure him—only give John more time with his family, and most important, more comfort.

On December 29, 1997, our ninth child was born, a lovely little girl.

On January 5, 1998, John did the hardest thing he had ever done. He left by bus for Florida with our 17-year-old daughter and John's brother who is married to my sister. He left the family behind, including the new baby and Mother who was on a recliner due to infected varicose veins.

In Lexington, Kentucky, John's cousin married to another of my sisters, joined them and went along to Florida. They traveled 36 hours to reach their destination. They were there one-and-one-half days till John had his treatment, then started home again. They were gone from Sunday night till Saturday evening. The trip was very hard on both John and me. He never wanted to leave me again. Very seldom did either of us go anywhere without the other after that.

John was seemingly healthy, and did most any kind of work on the farm, from riding a tractor to driving the team of horses on the haybine.

In early May, John started having light seizures. He was in and out of the hospital while they tried to adjust his medication dosage. By the end of May, John was having hard Grand Mal seizures many times a day. The MRI's showed a mass of what the doctors believed to be scarred tissue pressing on nerves. But it was lying on the motor skills' part in the center of his brain.

We contacted surgeons far and wide, but they did not want to attempt surgeries to give John relief. One local specialist told us outright, "No one can do anything. Take him home. Watch him die. When the pressure builds up so much, it will take his life."

Once again, we turned to the Florida surgeon who had been in contact with us all that time. He encouraged us to find a good surgeon closer to home. But we planned a quick trip to Florida. John was bedfast. On Monday, June 15, my sister Rhoda, our five-and-one-half month old baby girl, John (on a stretcher and transported by ambulance), and I boarded an ambulance jet called Care Flight at a local airport.

Care Flight had a wonderful Christian crew. The trip to Florida took two hours and forty-five minutes. John was scheduled to have an open-head surgery the next morning while he was awake. They took him to surgery at 5:00 a.m. Finally at 2:00 p.m. they came to the waiting room to talk to us. Eighty-five per cent of the mass was scar tissue and 15 per cent was the tumor regrowth. They removed 95 per cent of the mass. The rest was entwined around the motor skills part of his brain and was unremovable. John had a hard seizure during surgery. After that, his left side was paralyzed.

Finally, after twelve-and-one-half hours, we were reunited in John's room. He was very sick. During surgery he had felt them pulling and tugging on the tumor in his brain. The day following surgery he was still very ill. The doctor said, "One more seizure could take him."

John's emotional recovery was very slow. He never fully recovered physically. But the main thing was, he got relief from his constant seizures, and was fairly comfortable and without pain the rest of his days. He needed to take high dosages of medication.

Following this surgery, John was mostly in a wheel chair, although he did walk with my help. His left arm and hand was useless. He would get bored of sitting and being waited on when he wanted to work so badly. John often tried working with one hand, but that was too tiring for him. Oh, the precious memories of being together.

We were thankful for the many neighbors and friends who visited us. Visitors helped John get his mind off his own trials, thus encouraging him.

We did not attempt to attend church services till October 1998, when we attended several times. Although we did go to several other places that summer, being gone only for short times. By mid-October, we could see signs that John was losing out. How it hurt to see that the fight for life here on earth would soon be over for our loved one. By that time John was also resigned and remarked that he would like to stay with us, but he was weary of traveling this way.

On November 26 our oldest son, Lyle, was married to Alma Burkholder. We were so glad we could all attend the wedding. That seemed to be what John had lived for. From that time on he lost out fast. Wistfully, I thought perhaps the losing-out was from the flop he took out of the wheel chair.

The following Monday John was sick with pneumonia, which he fought for two weeks. These two weeks were very hard weeks for all of us. Thankfully, he felt better the last two weeks of his life and talked more with the children. He was more alert than he had been before the wedding.

On the evening of December 28, John had severe pain in the back of his neck and up toward his brain. We all came together and sang, as we thought this would probably be close to the end. After about an hour, he felt better again. We were so thankful that he didn't have seizures during that time. The following day, Tuesday, he seemed better and, of course, our hopes rose. But by evening John started with labored breathing. He was still able to carry on a conversation, but he needed to sit on a recliner so he could breathe. Wednesday morning he had a temperature of 105 degrees. That remained till his death. Wednesday evening we finally got oxygen and a suction machine for him. John had lots of phlegm. Our son, Lyle left work so the family could all be home. Kind neighbors and friends attended to our daily earthly cares, which really are so unimportant at times like this.

Thursday morning at breakfast time, John was hungry. His night had been about the same, but now he found he could no longer swallow. Oh, the heartache! We spent the day using a medicine dropper to wet his mouth, lips, and throat. We, as a family, spent most of the day in singing. That evening at seven o'clock his breathing relaxed and became more shallow. We knew John was fading away. Soon after that we realized the brain tumor was growing fast! A film-like scar tissue was pushing out over his right eye and he could no longer see with that eye. He still kept his left eye on my face. He also shook his head in response to the question of whether he had a headache.

Oh, those last precious moments... The children all gathered around for their last farewell. Then we sang one more song, "Oh, Sing To Me Of Heaven" in *The Christian Hymnal*. As we sang the third verse, "Oh watch my dying face..." John took his last shuddering breath at 8:28 p.m. on December 31, 1998. Our dear husband and father crossed over to that other side to a new and distant shore. And so we placed our loved one in our Heavenly Father's loving care.

The following day (New Year's Day) was very cold. Friends gathered at our home. By Saturday, a winter storm had set in, making roads nearly impassable. Sunday was a very stormy day, the worst winter storm we had for years. The decision was made to postpone the funeral till Tuesday. Monday the roads were still bad, but the storm had begun to let up. By Tuesday morning, the morning of the funeral, the temperature was twenty degrees below zero. Our bodies and minds felt almost frozen.

We have received many cards, letters, and poems. It is our desire to accept life as God had planned it for us, however hard and lonely it is.

—*Rachel Ramer*
Wakarusa, Indiana

CARL E. MARTIN
March 8, 1955 to May 28, 1988 (33 years)

When The Lord Called
Marlene Martin, Wife

On Friday, May 27, 1988, we as a family did our afternoon milking at 2:00. We were milking three times a day at that time. We would then milk at regular time in the morning. We were in partnership with my sister Alta and her husband, Stanley, who was Carl's cousin.

After milking the cows, we went to Shipshewana for the evening. Carl was on the Haiti board and there was a Haiti Benefit Auction planned for Saturday. We went to listen to the special singing and to look at all the things that would be sold the next day.

We didn't stay long because we were all tired from the day's work.

The next day, May 28, 1988, dawned as a normal day would. Little did we realize the change this day would bring to our lives.

Carl wanted to plant the last of the corn after the morning milking. This was a hay field we had just chopped and plowed, and needed to get it planted. They had been irrigating that hay field because we hadn't had much rain, so the hay hadn't grown very much. It seemed Carl was just too busy to be present at the Haiti auction.

We all ate breakfast together that morning, little realizing this would be the last time we would be together with our seven precious children: Janette (11), Rosetta (10), Patricia (8), Thelma (6), Alice (5), Harvey (three-and-one-half), and Carlton (one-and-one-half). I don't remember all of that morning's activity.

That was the day a widow, Sandra Eberly, was remarried in our church. We were all very happy for her. Since Sister Alta and Stanley were invited to the wedding, I had planned to take care of their four children. We were always glad to have them come. We were often together over chore time and the children had lots of fun playing with one another. So that Saturday we didn't get much housecleaning done.

That morning we picked our first strawberries. They tasted very good, but we didn't get very many. We knew we wouldn't get much of a crop if we didn't get rain.

When lunchtime came, Carl was working with the irrigation, so I made him several sandwiches for lunch and took them to the field. He said he wasn't very hungry and only ate one sandwich. He told me what all he was planning to do with the irrigation, and then I left because I needed to get back to my house full of children.

At 2:00 p.m., I took the children with me to the barn across the road where we did our milking. I left some of the children in the house over there. Charles Martins, (Stanley's parents), were living there. I took some of the girls with me to help chore.

The lights blinked off while we were choring. We all wondered, "What happened?" We figured it was some accident or something... We never dreamt it involved my dear husband.

Stanleys came home from the wedding and changed clothes. Stanley then wanted to go and see how Carl was coming along with the irrigating. He was at the neighbors' one-half mile away. The irrigation was set up along the lane. When they got there, they saw Carl was lying beside the lane. Stanley noticed he wasn't breathing, and quickly started doing CPR, while Alta ran to phone for help. She also called to the barn and told us that something was wrong with Carl. I quickly left the barn, wondering all the while what could be wrong.

The fire department, of which Carl was the assistant chief, soon arrived and continued to do CPR until the ambulance arrived. They shocked him to try to get his heart going again. I thought, "Good, I think I saw him breathe." Soon they told me to step back.

Many of my family came to see what had happened. They were trying to see what had caused it all. If he was sick, I had not known it. They thought maybe he had a heat stroke. Then someone discovered a mark on his shoulder. Looking at the irrigation pipe laying near him, they noticed it had an arc on it. With the electric line overhead, we soon decided he had lifted the pipe up to empty out the sand, which came from irrigating manure, and hit the wire.

My dear parents took me home to change clothes. My dear children were all there with many others who had come to be with them. My parents took me to the hospital.

There they took us to the chaplain's room. Carl's dear mother and sister came in, and oh, how the tears did flow! Minister Merle and Berdine Ramer were there to give their support, of which I was very thankful.

It seemed the time went very slow until we were finally able to see my companion. Oh, his form was so still and cold. I thought as Job did, *"The Lord has given and the Lord has taken away."* The question also came, "Why me, Lord? What will I do now?" The answer came, "The Lord will provide."

We sure felt His comforting presence in the days that followed.

We came home to a houseful of family and friends. The children were just sitting around with some of the family.

This happened Saturday afternoon. Visitation started Sunday afternoon. The undertakers thought it best to have the funeral as soon as possible because of Carl being burned so badly internally. Oh, it seemed too soon to have the funeral.

My parents stayed with us nights over the viewing and funeral.

Some of the children were very reluctant to see their daddy so still and quiet in a casket. Death is so final. Family and many friends came to show their sympathy. We were so grateful for all the love and kindness shown to us.

The morning of the funeral, I thought my dad should try to explain to the children about the burial. He used the illustration of our hand in a glove. He likened it to our bodies. Then he pulled out his hand and told the children, "That's what happens when we die. Our soul leaves and goes to God and we bury the outer part."

It was a very large funeral. I didn't realize there were so many people who cared about us. I was deeply encouraged knowing that everyone cared, but yet, I didn't know how I could go on.

After the funeral my parents and Carl's mom took turns staying with us nights. I was very grateful they did, but after some time I thought I should try to find a new normal for our lives, and with God's help try to go ahead.

(Carl's mother was special in various ways. His father chose to leave the family. So Carl's mother was left with the responsibility of rearing four young children. He lived with another woman, then died of cancer several years after Carl's death.)

Four months after Carl's death, God gave us a baby boy. We called him Edward Lee, but God chose that he should never have to live here on the earth. We were allowed to bury him right on top of his daddy's casket.

We never had the privilege to enjoy taking care of Baby Edward, but I feel his daddy is enjoying taking his hand and walking those streets of pure gold.

Following Carl's death, we continued helping on the dairy farm. The church assisted us financially.

After five years, we decided it would be best to find something we could do as a family. We were uncertain as to what it should be, and we asked the Lord for direction.

Things opened up for us to move to a chicken farm in June of 1993. We have 8,000 caged laying hens. We gather and candle the eggs. We plan to discontinue this business in the near future.

We also have a processing plant where we do custom chicken butchering. We started this three years ago, and the Lord has greatly blessed our business.

—*Marlene Martin & family*
Goshen, Indiana

Living In Trust

I cannot see what lies ahead,
Whether sunshine, pain or tears.
I'll live each day with faith in Him
Who wipes away all fears.
My Lord has promised to stand by
To guide and care for me;
I'll take each day and walk with Him
Down paths I cannot see.

-Author Unknown

"For I reckon that the sufferings of this present time
are not worthy to be compared with the glory which
shall be revealed in us" (Romans 8:18).

"...for He hath said I will never leave thee nor forsake thee" (Hebrews 13:5).

FREDA (TROYER) SCHLABACH
September 21, 1928 to June 22, 1996 (67 years)

Widowhood, Not An Easy Life
Moses A. Schlabach, Husband

Our wedded life began with a big snowstorm, high winds, and drifting snow on Thanksgiving Day, November 23, 1950.

In the next sixteen-and-one-half years there were eight children born to us: Katie, Edward, Bena, Paul, Emma, Reuben, Ruth, and Roy.

Freda and I were both fairly healthy until 1991 when Freda began to have problems. After receiving considerable encouragement from friends, we traveled to a medical center in Mexico.

By the following January 1992, Freda was admitted to the hospital in Ohio with pain in her left arm, apparently due to a blood clot. The next morning she was transferred to another hospital. That same day she suffered a stroke which affected her swallowing, speech, and balance. They began therapy, then transferred her to a therapy hospital.

The third week of Freda's hospital stay, I was taken to the hospital with a heart attack. Freda and I were now both in a hospital, but 30 miles apart.

After Freda was discharged from the hospital she could do most of her housework, although her balance wasn't back to normal. The grandchildren found it a challenge, and took much pride in helping Grandmother walk outside.

Since we both were somewhat on the handicapped side, we had farm sale. Then son Reuben and family took over the farm.

After 1992 we gave up some traveling, which we had enjoyed so much in the past.

In the spring of 1996 Freda said she thinks she would feel well enough to go on a Green Country Tour. These tours were always in the back of our minds.

Two years before, we had attended the Yoder School reunion of Limpytown. There was much interest shown in the school days gone by. So we were asked if we would want to make up a school book of our past school days. We consented. It took much effort, but we came up with an interesting book. We took it to the printers, and they told us it would be done by the week of June 17, 1996. That was just fine, as the school reunion was scheduled for June 22.

Now as you read on you will see the Good Lord had other plans for us that day. The saying goes, "We don't know the future, but we know Who holds the future." This became reality to us on Tuesday, June 18, 1996. The morning started off for us as usual. We got up at five o'clock. I was at the desk writing when Mother got out of bed and dressed herself saying she had slept well. Little did I realize then that this was her last night's rest in our bed.

Freda was sitting on the couch. Soon she said she felt dizzy, so I told her to go and get a drink of water. She stood up and said, "I can't even walk." That alarmed me. I quickly went over to help her, but she only slumped back onto the couch—unconscious. I fanned her for a little; then I went to find Reuben. I met him just as he was coming out of his house.

Reuben took one look at Mother and said, "We need to get help. I'll go call 911." The emergency squad soon came. They examined Freda, then put her on a stretcher and took her and me to the hospital. By then she had recovered a little, but she could not hold a conversation. I soon saw I needed someone for support, so I asked to have Paul and Reuben brought to the emergency room.

Freda was not very well and was admitted to the hospital. At 7:00 Paul and Reuben came, but Mother did not respond. We soon called for the rest of the children.

Katie and her husband were in Texas on a western trip, and Ruth and her husband were on a Smokey Mountain trip, but we got word to both.

Later in the day Freda seemed some better. She had a good hand grip, but she still couldn't talk. She did not make any improvement the next few days. We felt it surely can't be long till she will leave us and enter into eternity.

One by one we bid her good-by. This was a very touching experience, realizing we might have to give up our faithful Mother. She greatly loved our children and grandchildren. She was a faithful life partner. She often read God's Word and was a good example for me. I realized if she leaves, she would surely take part of me with her.

Thursday evening, June 20, Mother seemed very low. She was often checked by a nurse. Her brothers and sister were there with us. At seven o'clock she responded to our conversation. But by 8:30 p.m., she did not respond anymore. Since Mother was so low, the family stayed on. I appreciated that. Roy and Brenda came home at 11:00 p.m., and Jonas Rabers (daughter Katie) soon came, too.

Saturday, June 22, 1996, my companion was losing out. She was getting weaker and had much labored breathing. All our family was there when Freda took her last breath, except Bena.

When we were ready to leave the hospital, the funeral director came and we gave him some information for the memorial.

Now to go home without Mother and face the neighbors... At home we found people cleaning the barn and stables, weed-eaters were humming, food was being prepared, and the house cleaned. Many neighbors showed up to help prepare for the funeral of my life's partner of 45 years. The feeling was indescribable. What would we do if we wouldn't have kind neighbors?

The viewing was held on Sunday and Monday. The funeral day was June 25 with services held in the barn and in the house. It was a nice cool day, but the parting was not easy—no words can describe it. Freda's earthly body was laid to rest in the Miller Cemetery along Township Road 310.

I appreciated the many visitors after the funeral and in the years afterwards. The many cards and notes were like a healing balm.

Widow-hood

Widow-hood is not an easy life,
No matter is it man or wife,
You lay awake in the dark at night,
Hoping and wishing for more heavenly light.

And as you lay there and wonder,
Will the sun again come up yonder?

So you breathe a prayer to the heavenly throne,
The answer will be, "You are not alone."

This gives you a ray of hope,
Your adversary to cope.
I'll tell what visitors can do,
They smother the loneliness out of you.

Grieving cannot be easy explained,
Of what the body now has attained.
You are somewhat in a daze,
But those good memories you don't erase.

-Moses A.Schlabach

Much comfort can be had by relying on the Good Lord, and asking for His help and guidance.

After being a widower for three-and-one-half years, I contacted Anna Yoder and she agreed to come and share life's joys and sorrows with me.

Oh, *"the unsearchable riches of Christ;"* (Ephesians 3:8).

—Moses A. Schlabach
Millersburg, Ohio

"For we know that if our earthly house of this taber-nacle were dissolved, we have a building of God, an house not made with hands, eternal in the heavens" (II Corinthians 5:1).

A Bereaved's Life Experience
Moses A. Schlabach

What will become of a married life when a life partner is called into eternity? The change and shock can almost numb, or stun a person. It can almost put you in a daze. In a sense, you feel like you've had an amputation.

It helps to talk with someone who has traveled the road before.

The line between grief and self-pity is very thin, but life goes on regardless.

The sun still rises in the east and sets in the west—the world stays the same, but a widowed life has changed.

It helps to get inner peace by remembering the 23rd Psalm, and the marriage vow: *"Till death do us part."*

It is not easy to part with a partner that you have loved, and lived with, and with whom you shared life's sorrows and joys.

From experience you can tell that if people just drop in for a short visit that it helps to see the light at the end of the tunnel.

A widowed person is more or less thrust out of their normal, down-to-earth way of thinking, similar to going into outer-space with timeless unanswered questions. Then about the time we feel we have things fairly well under control, a wave of emotions spills over us.

We must accept this change of a lifestyle. It demands great effort to plow through one stage of mourning into the next.

The price of wholeness is courage, and the price is not too high. Peace and joy can be found in spite of the emptiness you now feel.

We must not feel as if we have lost something incredible or wonderful that should have been ours for always.

We must recognize that death is just another step in God's plan for our life, and accept the life-death cycle as common to all creation.

Allow yourself sufficient time to let grieving take its course.

Forget about becoming your 'old self' again. Renew your faith in God and yourself. It will make you an even better person capable both of loving and of living normally again.

Learn to accept people if they are not as you would like them to be.

Try to come to a full discovery of yourself as an individual, as a complete person capable of looking to your own needs and desires, and of controlling and coming to grips with your emotions.

Work to overcome boredom and self-pity. To break the routine, start creating new interests and accepting the help of others as you come to recognize your own individual self-worth and self-esteem.

Then you can, as one who has come through the grief of widowhood, share your strength, faith, hope, and experience with others who are still struggling with their grief.

We must now change from our past life of experience to the fond life of memories, and then use our God-given talent to start a new journey in life. This can enkindle great thoughts. This can help us to endure loneliness and grief when it comes upon us full-force. Then for more comfort we must pour our heart out to the Lord and ask for more of His guidance and help.

—*Moses A. Schlabach*
Millersburg, Ohio

He Maketh No Mistake

My Father's way may twist and turn,
My heart may throb and ache;
But in my soul I'm glad I know
He maketh no mistake.

My cherished plans may go astray,
My hopes may fade away;
But still I'll trust my Lord to lead,
For He doth know the way.

Tho' night be dark and it may seem
That day will never break,
I'll pin my faith, my all, in Him;
He maketh no mistake.

There's so much now I cannot see,
My eyesight far too dim;
But come what may, I'll simply trust
And leave it all to Him.

For bye and bye the mist will lift,
And plain it all He'll make.
Through all the way, tho' dark to me,
He made not one mistake!
-*Author Unknown*

DENNIS SANDLIN
July 1, 1960 to January 25, 2000 (39 years)

Some Day We'll Never Say Good-by
Cherie Sandlin, Wife

"The Lord has given and the Lord has taken away. Blessed be the name of the Lord" (Job 1:21).

A great man has died. He wasn't a world leader or a famous doctor, or a war hero, or a sports figure. He was no business tycoon, and you would never see his name in the financial pages. But he was one of the greatest men that ever lived. He was my husband and the father of my children. I guess you might say he was a person who was never interested in getting credit or receiving honors. He treated his job like his own business, and often worked when he should have been at home in bed. He liked doing things like going to church, helping the children with homework, and playing games with them. His favorite song was "I Need No Mansion Here Below," and he didn't need one to be happy. He was a great success as husband, father, son, son-in-law, and friend. I wonder how many millionaires can say that. As my best friend and husband he has been greatly missed.

Dennis and I were married October 5, 1979. I would never have thought I would have to give him up after 20 years of marriage. I still agree with the saying, "Tis better to have loved and lost, than never to have loved at all."

Our children are: Chad Michael, 1980; Conrad Lee, 1982; Julie Ann, 1985; and Cara Nicole, 1988. Dennis was a carpenter, so we lived in several new houses. In 1983 work was scarce, so we moved to Salisbury, Maryland. We were there for three years then moved back to Elida, Ohio.

In March of 1994, I finally talked Dennis into getting a mole checked that was on his left hip. The skin specialist said he didn't think it was anything and didn't need to take it off. Dennis told him to go ahead and take it off because I kept bugging him about it. Less than a week later they called and said it was a 3.7 melanoma cancer. He set up an appointment with a doctor in Columbus. They did CAT scans and scheduled him for surgery a week later. Dennis wanted anointing before surgery. That really meant a lot to us. On April 15, 1994, they took out 11 lymph nodes and two of them tested positive. He was in the hospital five days. I slept by his side so I could care for him.

The next three years were uneventful. He had CAT scans and we never really worried about the cancer coming back. We were both more optimistic in nature. We got to the place where we didn't even call to see what the results of the scans were. He had CAT scans again in February 1997, and when we didn't hear anything a month later we assumed everything was okay.

What a shock it was when we got a call in April that the cancer was back. The doctor wanted us to come to Columbus to talk with him. Dennis' appointment was on my 38th birthday. Dennis said no matter what we find out we're going to celebrate. The report was worse than we ever thought it would be and we just sat there and didn't say anything. The doctor said: "You do understand the seriousness of this situation don't you?" We both said, "Yes."

They set Dennis up for an MRI to make sure the cancer hadn't spread to his brain. Well, we went out to the car and I was sitting up against him and tears started running down my face. I didn't want him to see me though. As we were going down the road, he happened to look down at me and said, "I told you we were going to celebrate." I just burst out crying and told him, "You're not the one that would be left." One week later the brain scan came back clear. We were so thankful.

The next 11 months went fairly smooth, except for trying some diets which Dennis hated. They could have tried operating, but the doctor said it would have been a very difficult operation. Dennis said he would rather die than go through another operation like the last one.

April 1998, Dennis was taping out some drywall. He got down, came over, and sat in a chair. I asked him what was the matter. He couldn't say the words he wanted—they were all mixed up. When he stood up, he had a seizure. Oh, how scary that was! I thought he was dying. The rescue squad was called and I went with them to take Dennis to the hospital. That is when we found out the cancer had gone to his brain. The doctor gave him three to four months to live.

In July 1998, a friend of ours gave us papers about a doctor that seemed to be helping a lot of people in the Dominican Republic. That was the hardest decision we ever made. But my husband decided that is what he wanted to do. So there we were on a plane headed for the Dominican, and we didn't know anyone.

One of the doctor's helpers met us at the airport. He couldn't speak English, and we couldn't speak Spanish. He held up a sign with Dennis Sandlin on it, and also held a note from the doctor. The man took us to a motel where someone could at least halfway talk to us. They would pick us up and take us to the clinic every day. We didn't have a car, so we had to walk everywhere we went. There was no laundry. I washed our clothes in the sink or tub. Dennis had a seizure while we were there, and didn't know who I was, or where he was, for about an hour. I was so thankful when that month was up.

We went there again in September. This time we were only going to be there one week, so we took Conrad along to help us. Then in October Dennis was scheduled to go to the Dominican Republic again. I was having a large bake sale, so Chad and Edwin (nephew) went with Dennis. They were gone nine days. When he came home, he said some of the most beautiful words to me. He said, "I'm never going again without you. The last couple of days, all I could think of was you."

October 30, I had a big bake sale. Chad stayed with Dennis while I went to the sale. That week Dennis was having bad headaches. I came home from the sale at 5:00 p.m. and he wanted to go out to eat with our friends that have the sales with us. He ate heartily that night, but was sometimes hard to understand.

Sunday his headache was worse. Doctor _____, a member of our church, agreed to be his doctor. She ordered pain patches to help control the pain, so I sent my oldest son for the prescription. It seemed like it was taking longer than it should have. My husband was in great pain and kept wondering where Chad was. Then the phone rang. It was Chad saying I should come get the pain medication, because he had totaled his car. He had gone over the railroad tracks too fast and hit a tree. The first thing he said when I arrived was, "Well, Mom, at least the motor's still good."

That afternoon the doctor said she thought it was time to get hospice to help us. She checked Dennis and said the tumor either shifted, or there was another one. (He already had three tumors in his brain.)

By the time hospice came out, Dennis was in so much pain, he hardly knew what was going on. Hospice wanted me to fill out papers, but I said I wouldn't do anything till they got his pain under control. Hospice didn't have any pain medication with them, so Conrad and I drove up to the hospital and picked it up. When we arrived home, they gave him morphine. Fifteen minutes later, they gave him more. Nothing worked. He started vomiting bile and wasn't comprehending anything around him. We called the doctor and she told us to call the rescue squad.

When we got to the hospital, they again wanted to take care of paperwork. I told them I would take care of paperwork after they gave him pain medication. They said they had to know something about him to be able to help him. I told them that all they needed to know was that he had a melanoma brain tumor and he was in pain! I guess they knew I was serious. They started giving him pain medication, but it still was not helping. The doctor later told me, he had a friend who died of melanoma, and he died screaming. (That was not reassuring!) Dennis never screamed, but he would hold his head. Once he said, "Why does anyone have to have this much pain?"

Chad stayed with him all that night. I could not stand to be with him long—he was in so much pain. The next morning we had to make a decision about whether to transfer Dennis to a larger hospital for an operation, or let him go. The doctor really gave him no hope. I felt life had almost ended for him, and that I should let him go. My sons just couldn't seem to let him go, so I had the bishop of our church, my brother, and the boys make the decision. They decided, for the boys' sake, they would transfer him. My oldest son went with Dennis in the rescue squad. My brother took Dennis' parents and me in his van. We knew we couldn't keep up with the rescue squad, so it was quite a shock when we came upon it sitting by the side of the road about halfway to the hospital. A belt had broken and all the transmission fluid had drained out. We had to wait an hour for another rescue squad to come. After we were on our way we saw a large sign that said, "TRUST JESUS." That was really encouraging to me.

When we arrived at the hospital, Conrad went to the restroom and came back with a tract he had found with "TRUST" written in big letters across the top. The following poem was inside it.

Do you walk through the valley of shadows, my friend?
Do you suffer depression and pain?
Do you think God forgets you and leaves you alone
To bear your own burden and shame?

Well, I walk the same road you're going—and yes,
At times I can't see light for the gray.
I'd stumble and fall if it were not for Jesus
Who knows every step of my way.

He puts me in shadows so I cannot find
The pathway by my sight alone.
Through faith He has saved me, through faith He now
    guides me;
Yet not on my strength, but His own!

He moves in strange ways that I would not choose,
Through darkness and gloom and despair.

No matter how hopeless, believe on Him, friend,
For Jesus is always there.

-*Tim Harvey*

Dennis was at this hospital less than an hour till they had his pain under control. I went to be by his side in the emergency room. His first words asked were where the girls were and who was taking care of them. Julie had come with us, so she went back to see him.

The doctor then talked to me. He was very upbeat about Dennis having surgery. He said there were risks involved, but he felt he could have some good years yet. They wanted to get the swelling down before surgery. After waiting a few days, they operated on November 4, 1998. They took him to surgery at 7:30 a.m., and called me back to see him at 11:30 a.m. You wouldn't have known by talking to Dennis that anything had happened. He was back to his old self. He was in the hospital till Sunday, and of course, I slept by his side.

He went back to work three weeks later. Chad worked with him, so it worked out really well. Chad could do the driving. One day they came rushing home, and Dennis was driving. Chad came in, blood running down his face. He had been drilling through a roof and the drill slipped and hit his eyelid and cheek. I took him to the medical center where they put a stitch in his eyelid. We were so glad it missed his eye.

Dennis was getting along really well, so the doctors decided to try a new procedure called the gamma knife. He still had two other tumors that they didn't get with surgery.

On April 15, 1998, he had the gamma knife done, and got along really well. He was kept overnight because it was a new procedure for the hospital.

We arrived home on Saturday. Then on Sunday I started with gallbladder attacks. (I had gallbladder surgery one month after Dennis passed away.)

That summer went really well, except for Dennis having seizures every so often. He would bite his tongue during the seizures, and it would hurt him so badly. I told him it hurt me just as much as him. He said, "You don't realize how much it hurts." He usually kept his sense of humor through it all. Once I tried to stick the corner of a book in his mouth when he started into a seizure. Later he said, "Maybe it would have gone into your mouth, but not mine."

In August, we took a trip with the children to Missouri, and had a nice time. That was the last trip with the family all along.

October 5, 1999, was our 20th wedding anniversary. My sister-in-law had a wonderful party for us and we so enjoyed the fellowship. They sang some of the songs we had at our wedding.

In November, Dennis' leg started hurting, so I took him to the medical center. Doctor ___ sent us to the hospital for an ultrasound on his leg. They discovered a blood clot, and kept him in the hospital. They put him on Coumidin, which needed to be checked at the hospital twice a week. He was there over Thanksgiving. While there, Julie came down with the flu. Dennis called the florist shop, and had flowers delivered to the house for her.

December 10, he had a gamma knife again. More tumors were growing. This time they did it as an outpatient, so we went home that evening. We hardly made it in the driveway till he said to stop the car. He got out and vomited several times. He was sick that whole weekend, so my brother, Rick, took Dennis and me to the emergency room. They kept him overnight, then sent him home with medication for nausea. It didn't seem to help much, and he couldn't keep much down after that.

December 17, Dennis asked me to bring him the phone book. He said he wanted to order flowers for his other daughter, Cara. When they were delivered, here I discovered he had ordered flowers for me, too. On the card it said, "Thanks for taking good care of me." Those flowers and the card were really special to me.

That evening was the Christmas program at school. The girls wanted him to be there so much, so we went right after it started. We sat at the back of the room and he put his leg up on another chair. Sweat just ran down his face, so I fanned him all evening. We left just as they stood to close so he wouldn't have to stand and talk to people.

We had the Sandlin Christmas get-together on December 18, at our house. Dennis had always helped me when we had company, and it was very hard for him just to sit and watch me. He asked me if there was cleaning he could help me with while sitting.

Dennis didn't eat out at the table with us. He came out after we were finished and sat in his chair. I fixed him a plate. He didn't eat much. We had our gift exchange and he stayed in the room with us till everyone went home.

The next week, we had my side of the family for a Christmas dinner. Dennis was feeling worse then, but he was with us for the gift exchange. Saturday, the 25th, the girls came into our room and woke us, wanting to get on with Christmas. We woke up the boys and went to the living room to read the Christmas story, and then open gifts. Dennis stayed with us till after the gifts were all opened, then went to lie down. Dennis told me he was sorry he didn't feel like staying in the living room. I told him we all understood.

Dennis didn't go to church on Sunday. And Monday his speech was slurred. So, I called to the doctor's office and they said to call the rescue squad and get him checked out. It turned out that they had his Coumidin level dangerously high and one of the tumors was hemorrhaging. He was transferred to the larger hospital again. This time I went with him in the rescue squad.

At the hospital they gave me a cot by his bed part of the time, and the rest of the time I slept by his bed in a chair. Kind friends would bring me clothes and take my dirty ones home to wash them. We were so thankful for the many friends that came to visit us in those, seemingly, long weeks.

Dennis' doctor was in Paris, so the brain surgeon was the main doctor. When his doctor got back, they had just put a direct line in to feed him. But his doctor said it was just feeding the cancer. We decided to go home since they could do no more.

Just before we left, the doctor came in and told Dennis, "I'm not going to say you're not going to get well, you've already surprised us. There's just nothing more we can do." That was January 14, 2000. We had celebrated the New Year in the hospital.

Rick flew his plane to Columbus to get us. We were thankful for the short trip home. Hospice was at our house when we got home, waiting to hook up the pain medication.

The following Monday Dennis had a seizure. Wednesday night he was up and down all night with me trailing him with the pain medication. He got his pain medication through a needle that was placed just under the skin on his stomach. He could also press a button every 15 minutes if he needed more.

Our boys were in Bible school. Thursday morning hospice said to call them to come home right away or they would never get to talk to their dad again. I called them and they left for home right away. Dennis still thought he might get well. So I hated to tell him that hospice said he probably would not last the weekend. I knew with the boys coming home, he would wonder. When he asked me why the boys were coming home, I told him hospice said he could go into a coma at any time, and if the boys wanted to talk to him, they should come home. He asked, "How long do I have?" I said, "Do you really want to know?" He said, "No."

After I had talked to him, he wanted me to call the ministers for another anointing. He said, not to get well exactly, but he just felt he could give up better if he had an anointing. So Thursday evening we had the anointing service. When they asked if their was any sin in his life, he said he had thrown a brick at a mailbox once, and wanted to make that right. He had told me years earlier, and I was going to write the letter for him, but had never gotten it done. I told him I would do it right away. I wrote to them and told them he was sorry and sent them $20. They sent back a wonderful letter of forgiveness and the money. Dennis died before we got the letter, but somehow, I think he knows.

The boys arrived home later that evening. Dennis' unsaved brother was there too. In the hospital Dennis had told me he hoped he would get a chance to talk to his brother about his soul. He got a chance to talk to him that night. The next morning Conrad came into his room and told him to squeeze his hand as hard as he could.

Conrad said it hurt. As he went out Dennis said, "I love you, Conrad."

Every February, we had a Valentine's party for all the couples in the church that were married in the 70's. When he was in the hospital, Dennis said he wanted to live to attend that party. They had the party the Saturday before he died, because my sister was here from Puerto Rico. They all brought the party to him. They brought the centerpiece of roses to us, and then stood around his bed and sang. It was a very touching scene and meant so much to us.

On Sunday my brother-in-law came and shaved Dennis for me, and read Psalm 23 to him. He also gave Dennis his shot. He had to have a shot twice a day. It was terribly hard for me to give it, even though Dennis didn't mind it. He had given them to himself up until Thursday.

Monday evening, I was in bed by him and leaned over him. He put his arm around me and said, "I love you." Those were his last words. We just slept together in our bed. I could hold his hand and know at a moment's notice if something was wrong. We had a monitor though, and Chad took the other part to his room. All I had to say was, "Chad," and he was there. Monday night the doctor said she didn't see how he could possibly make it through the night. Chad came up and slept on the floor of our bedroom, and Dennis had a very restless night. He vomited bile several times and we were up changing bedding and washing sheets. I don't know what I would have done without Chad. The next morning when hospice came, they said the nurse that had come the night before had cut Dennis' pain medication in half. Hospice wasn't too happy about it, and I wasn't either.

I was so tired and had a terrible headache. I just thought I had to get some rest. My mother-in-law and

Dennis' Aunt Wanda, who was a nurse, came and sent me to get some sleep. I slept from 12:00 noon to 4:00 p.m. I woke up feeling much better, and the headache was gone. I was so thankful, because Dennis passed away that evening at 8:00. He went so peacefully with his family all around him. We had a Yoder's tape playing, which we liked so well. And just as he took his last breath, they were singing, "As I step on the beautiful shore."

At the viewing, I had pictures of different ones of the family holding his hand and a poem that said:

> *The clock of life is wound but once*
> *and no man has the power,*
> *To tell just when the clock will stop*
> *at late or early hour.*
> *Now is the only time you own;*
> *live, love, toil with a will.*
> *Place no faith in tomorrow*
> *for the clock may then be still.*

> *-Author Unknown*

It has been a little over a year now since Dennis has been gone. We still miss him, but our memories of him live on. We talk about him a lot. I think that really helps.

I found a framed poem that means a lot to me. This poem is where I got the title for my story:

We'll Never Say Goodbye

> *I cannot see you with my eyes*
> *or hear you with my ears,*
> *But thoughts of you are with me still*
> *and often dry my tears.*

You whisper in the rustling leaves
that linger in the fall
And in the gentle evening breeze
I'm sure I hear you call.
A part of you remains with me
that none can take away,
It gives me strength to carry on
at dawning of new day.
I think of happy times we shared
and then I softly sigh,
But this I know – we'll meet again
and never say goodbye.

-Larry Howland

—Cherie Sandlin
Elida, Ohio

"As one whom his mother comforteth, so will I comfort you" (Isaiah 66:13).

MERLE RAMER
April 3, 1952 to March 6, 1992 (39 years)

In Memory of Merle
Berdine Ramer, Wife

Merle died March 6, 1992 at the age of 39 years. He had suffered six years from the ravaging affects of a brain tumor. Surviving are his wife, Berdine, three sons, and one daughter. Merle was ordained minister in 1982 for the Wisler Mennonite Church.

"Help Me Lord" my feeble voice is calling
My life, my dreams are being swept away.
The earthly towers that I've built are falling
And sorrows mount with every passing day.

"Tell Me Lord" the answers to life's questions
My human mind in weakness wonders, "Why"?
I would not heed the devil's mean suggestions
Although my thoughts in desperation lie.

"Teach Me Lord" to wait upon your power
When pain and sickness rob me of my own.
That even in the darkest mortal hour
I feel the strength of thy immortal throne.

"Show Me Lord" the path that I should follow
To reach the place you've chosen out for me.
Forbid that I in pity here should wallow
When you have loftier things for me to see.

"Save Me Lord" when earthly storm clouds lower
When tempests buffet till my heart would faint.
Come calm the storm that I may view your power
And find the peace you've promised to the saint.

"Take Me Lord" when earthly life has ended
To dwell with those whose lives no ill can harm.
Where happy souls by angel hosts attended
Rest in the Father's everlasting arms.

-Dean Martin, Maryland

Cancer Is So Limited

It cannot cripple love-
It cannot shatter hope-
It cannot corrode faith-
It cannot eat away peace-
It cannot destroy confidence-
It cannot kill friendship-
It cannot shut out memories-
It cannot silence courage-
It cannot invade the soul-
It cannot reduce eternal life-
It cannot quench the Spirit-
It cannot lessen the power of the Resurrection-
Cancer Is So Limited

-Author Unknown

EDWARD N. GOOD
December 5, 1941 to August 16, 1963 (21 years)

ALDA (HACKERT) MARTIN
March 5, 1933 to March 25, 1966 (33 years)

In Memory of Our Loved Ones
David & Vera Martin, Husband & Wife

Edward and I were married on January 27, 1962. After a wedding trip filled with precious memories, we moved into a trailer on my parents' farm. In addition to a part time job, Edward helped my father on the farm. I worked in a factory.

Later, we were able to move to a rented farm and were kept busy with livestock and farming.

One Friday, August 16, 1963, I was busy with four baskets of peaches, and also, caring for our ten-month-old son, Leonard. I felt very busy, so my sister Anna Mary came to help. Edward came into the house to say that he's going to get a broken tractor part fixed. So he left. I, never thinking those would be his last words to me, went about my work.

I was doing my own canning for the first time and needed a rack to put into the bottom of my canner. So I called Laura, my brother Adam's wife. They lived on the next farm. She said she'd bring one over and would also stay to help with the peaches. But before she left she received another phone call... Adams were to bring me to the hospital. Edward was in a bad accident.

Laura stayed with Anna Mary and Leonard while Adam took me to the hospital. On the way, I kept hoping that I'd be able to talk to Edward. As we drove into the hospital parking lot, Edward's brother Moses was standing there waiting for us.

One look at his face told me that Edward was gone. I really wished I could see Edward, but they thought I shouldn't. They felt I wouldn't want that memory to haunt me.

Edward had been making a left-hand turn off the highway. A tractor-trailer truck driver didn't see Edward's turn signal in time and plowed into the back of the car, pushing him into the lane of oncoming traffic. Edward was thrown out of his car and broke his neck, which caused instant death.

As we drove home from the hospital, I felt so weak. "Why me?" kept going through my thoughts. We were only twenty-one years old and had been married only a year and a half. I didn't know anyone else who had lost a partner when they were so young.

I wasn't home very long before our neighbor Mrs. Adam Stauffer came over. She told me that she was about my age when she lost her husband—Here was someone who had had a similar experience. She will never know how much her words helped me. I believe she was sent to me by God.

Edward's family soon came, then funeral arrangements needed to be made. Edward's father had died four years earlier of a massive stroke. So his family was facing tragedy again. Edward was the youngest in a family of nine boys and two girls.

His brothers were all sitting in a row, when ten-month-old Leonard toddled down the row. He looked at each one, but couldn't find his daddy. Oh, how our hearts ached...

Edward and I had planned to have his family come for Sunday dinner—the first time they would all gather in our home—but God called them to come on Friday.

We had the viewing at home. As family and friends came to view the still form I could hardly grasp the reality that life would never be the same again.

That night after the viewing, Leonard just cried. I didn't know what was wrong. Thinking he might be missing his daddy, I took him to the coffin to show him his daddy's face. But it just didn't seem right to Leonard. His daddy didn't talk to him. Thinking of my son growing up without his daddy nearly broke my heart.

I don't know what I would have done without our loving Father to comfort me. Family and friends who helped out and prayed for me were also appreciated.

Four weeks prior to this Edward had been in a similar accident. That time when the phone rang, I was almost afraid to answer it. Somehow my intuition warned, "Something happened." I was so relieved when I heard Edward's voice asking me to come pick him up for the truck couldn't be driven. At that time I had to wonder how it would be if the accident had been fatal. I believe God was trying to prepare me for the real trial which was ahead.

Shortly after the funeral, I realized I was expecting our second child. Since I couldn't handle the farming, we sold the equipment and I moved back to my parents.

Leonard was a great comfort to me. I would show him pictures of his daddy and tell him we want to meet Daddy in heaven someday. The scripture verses on widows and the fatherless became special to me.

On May 23, 1964, Edward Jr. was born. He automatically received his father's name. I chose to have this baby at home. I felt I couldn't handle my emotions when other husbands would come to visit their wives and newborns at the hospital.

Now I had two sons to raise. Sometimes this seemed to be quite a load to carry, but they did help to fill the aching void in my heart. The songs, "How Far Is Heaven" and "No, Never Alone" became precious to me.

I started working in the factory again, trying to make ends meet. My sisters who were still at home enjoyed the boys greatly. They had Edward walking at seven months. Also, at this time I was hospitalized with appendicitis. Sharing the room with Edward's mother, who had had a heart attack, was very special to me.

Here is a poem someone sent to me:

Called Home

Dear Edward has been called away,
From family, friends, and home.
He left his darling little son,
And bosom companion alone.

Yet not alone God by your side,
Who has taken him away
Has promised never to forsake,
He'll be your strength and stay.

He left his home that Friday morn'
To be about his task.
Shall we ask if it was on his mind,
That this would be his last?

It may be that God had led
His thoughts to yonder shore

When traveling on that highway
Then quickly closed the door.

From Mother, Brothers, Sisters dear,
He took the youngest one.
Had He asked us which to take
He knew we would say none.

But God knows best and we would say
Thine will be done, not ours.
He sends such trials along our way
As thorns amid the flowers.

And when that final day shall break,
And God will call us home.
May we so live that we can meet,
Our loved ones around the throne.

There where there'll be no accidents,
No partings, nor sad good-bys.
There we shall all live permanent
In the home beyond the skies.

Time does have a way of healing. Three years later David S. Martin asked for my friendship.

He was a widower, having been married to Alda Hackert on November 26, 1953.

Alda had become diabetic at a young age and was sick a lot. Then on April 26, 1955, God blessed them with a baby girl. They named their bundle of joy Marian. As she grew, she had such a cute laugh.

In August, Marian had a bad cold, so they took her to the doctor. The doctor prescribed medicine and felt the baby would be all right. The next day, August 18, 1955, Baby Marian seemed worse, so they called for the doctor to come, but before he arrived Marian went into convulsions and died in her daddy's arms. She died of Baby Pneumonia at the age of four months.

This was very hard for David and Alda, as due to Alda's health problems, the doctor felt they shouldn't have more children. Alda helped fill her empty arms with helping care for her sister's children.

Over the years Alda needed to be hospitalized frequently. Her resistance to infections and colds was too low.

In March of 1966, David took Alda to the hospital again, not realizing that this would be the last time. She had pneumonia. One evening she asked to be anointed. So David called the ministry and they made plans to come in the morning. But Alda died that morning, March 25, 1966, before either David or the ministers had arrived. No one had realized that the end was so near.

This was a great trial for David. Now he was alone on a dairy farm. David was grateful for the help of family and friends. His brother, Clayton, lived next door and Rachel, Clayton's wife, sent many meals over for her brother-in-law. David's sister Elizabeth regularly did his housecleaning. And so life went on.

David and I were married on February 26, 1967. After an enjoyable trip to Florida, we were ready to head home to be with Leonard and Edward, who had stayed with my parents.

This was starting a new chapter, with many adjustments, in our lives. As time moved on, David and I were blessed with a daughter and three more sons.

We have felt the presence of God through all our experiences and know that we have been drawn closer to

Him because of our trials. Our thoughts are often on that home over there. We are more aware that we need to be ready, for we know not when our call will come.

"God is our refuge and strength, a very present help in trouble" (Psalm 46:1).

—David & Vera Martin
Lititz, Pennsylvania

"For our light affliction, which is but for a moment, worketh for us a far more exceeding and eternal weight of glory; While we look not at the things which are seen, but at the things which are not seen: for the things which are seen are temporal; but the things which are not seen are eternal" (II Corinthians 4:17-18).

JERRY ALAN HOOVER
June 11, 1956 to September 23, 1996 (40 years)

Farewell Jerry
Susan Hoover, Wife

"Hurry," Jerry said, "I need this to be faxed as soon as possible." We did not have a fax machine and I needed to go to my uncle's place to send the fax. As I was digging in my purse for the keys, I came across a piece of paper Jerry would need.

"Here's your permit," I said as I tossed the paper on the table in front of him. It never entered my mind that those would be the last words he would hear me say. I flew out the door, five-year-old Melissa in tow.

I had trouble sending the fax, eventually discovering that Jerry had given me the wrong number. In the meantime my uncle, Tillman Bear, received a funny fax and we had a good time laughing about it. At last my fax went through and I turned to leave. "Oh, one more thing," I said to Uncle Tillman, "I need a phone number from you." He gave me the number and I left.

About three-quarters of a mile from home I saw in my rear view mirror that Uncle Tillman was in his vehicle and trying to flag me down. I pulled over and he came up to the van. "You need to go to the bank," he said, "Jerry is in trouble." I looked at him carefully. "Are you serious?" He was.

Wondering what was wrong, I headed to the bank. What kind of trouble could Jerry be having? I couldn't imagine that he needed me for anything financial. What else could it possibly be? Oh, maybe he had a wreck at the corner. That reasoning made the most sense to me, but when I pulled up to the stop sign, I could see the van he used for his plumbing and electrical business sitting undamaged in a parking space. I was just clueless.

Uncle Tillman pulled in behind me and told me I should go in. "Like this?" I asked, suddenly conscious of the old dress and shabby sandals I had on. The bank vice-president and the receptionist met us inside. Very soberly they told me Jerry had passed out and was taken to the medical center by the rescue squad, and that I should go there. Uncle Tillman offered to go with me, but I thought I would rather have him take Melissa back to stay with my mom. I could envision being at the hospital for a while, and thought she would be happier at Grandma's house.

I fairly flew the seven miles to the medical center. About a mile from the hospital it suddenly occurred to me that Jerry could die. I went into a panic, and I started telling God how much we still needed him. Zipping around trying to find a parking space close to the door, I wasted time checking out three parking lots before I finally pulled into a space.

At the emergency room desk, I told the woman who I was and that the paramedics had just brought my husband in. She said she would see if he was there yet. She was gone a long time, and I paced the floor. Finally she came back and told me that they had brought someone else in who was in worse shape than my husband, and that person was given priority. That calmed me, but only for a moment.

I paced around looking for a clock and not knowing what to do with myself. The employee offered me coffee, but I wouldn't have been able to swallow it. I could feel people in the waiting room looking at me, but I couldn't sit down or stand still, and I couldn't find a clock. For some reason it seemed terribly important to know what time it was, but I had forgotten to put on my watch that morning.

After what seemed like a long time, a chaplain showed me to a small room. She prayed with me and asked if she could call anyone for me. I told her she could call my bishop, John Brunk. Unknown to me, my mom was not home, so my uncle found my father and left Melissa with him. When Pop heard what had happened, he headed to the hospital, but first stopped at home so Melissa could get some better clothes for me. It was sweet of her to think of that, but I never took them out of the bag.

A nurse came into the little room and explained what they were doing with Jerry, which didn't make me feel any better. She said something about his heart but I remember only that it didn't sound too encouraging. She also said a doctor would come in shortly and tell me more. Before long a big, tall doctor and a string of three or four nurses came in and sat down. The doctor began to explain to me what had happened, but the only thing that registered was "and he has expired." I burst into tears, but needed to make sure I really heard what I thought I had, and asked, "Do you mean he died?" The doctor said, "Yes." I started crying again, and I never knew the doctor and nurses left the room. The chaplain stayed with me and I asked her to call John and tell him that Jerry had died.

Someone asked if I'd like to see Jerry and I said, "Yes." They warned me that he would still have tubes in his mouth, but I didn't care. He was already cold. It was just unbelievable. I stayed in that room a long time, not wanting to leave. Time ceased to exist as a lifetime of memories washed over me. Pop arrived and held my hand as we cried together. John came with tears too.

Someone asked if I would allow him to be a tissue donor. I agreed, and we went through that process. I knew I had to leave sometime, but it was hard to walk out of that room and away from Jerry's body. We were handed Jerry's personal things; Pop carried the bag of clothes, and I took his boots.

Melissa had been in the care of some kind nurses and she was smiling when I went to get her. Pop and I each took a hand of hers and she chatted merrily; we were silent. After we got outside, she asked me why I had Papa's boots, and I told her he didn't need them anymore. That satisfied her until we got in the van. Then, sensing something was wrong, she asked why Papa wasn't coming with us. I told her I had something to tell her, and pulled her onto my lap. It's a very difficult thing to tell your child that her Papa has died.

We had Uncle Tillman and Aunt Elaine bring the school children home. They sat with my parents and me as I told Joel (15); Ryan (13); William (11); and Lynelle (6), the events of the morning. Uncle Tillman prayed with us. We sat crying, or in stunned silence, until I suddenly thought of calling Jerry's parents, Arthur and Gladys Hoover, in Wisconsin. News like this travels fast and I called them only moments before someone asked them if it was true that Jerry had died.

Our daughter, Jessica (17), was in Puerto Rico visiting friends and I had to call her there. It was a terrible experience to give her that kind of news by phone. She flew to Cleveland the next day. Since that is four hours from us by car, Rick Good offered to fly me there to pick her up. I was very grateful for his offer.

We waited until Friday to have the funeral so that Jerry's sister in Germany could come. I was not aware of much that went on that week. I found out later that someone had painted my garage doors. People were very kind in many ways, even taking our laundry away and doing it for us. One woman said she would stop in to drop something off when she went to pick up her children at school, and I had forgotten all about school—thinking the whole world had stopped when mine did.

The funeral was huge. I felt like I was in a play or something. I did whatever I was told to do. I ate and slept little all week. By the time Friday morning rolled around, it was starting to wear on me. I nearly passed out before the funeral started, and during the service I had to fight to either stay awake, or stay conscious. I couldn't decide which.

Jerry died of ventricular fibrillation. He had no history or complaint of heart trouble, but the night before he died he told me that ever since he had become overheated in the motel attic where he had been working six weeks before, he had not been able to get his energy back. He had been sick for a week after that incident, but he seemed to have gotten over most of it. The autopsy showed he had had a heart attack at some previous time. He never complained of pain, but looking back, I think that previous attack almost had to have happened the day he was overheated. The boys said he didn't "act right" on the way home that day. I lived with guilt and questions for a long time. Finally I came to realize that I had to lay it all down. I could not change what had happened.

After Jerry died, Lynelle and Melissa refused to sleep in their own bed and crawled into mine. I couldn't sleep that first night anyway, but as time went on it became a problem. I could hardly sleep with two little girls flopping around, so after they were asleep, I would carry one of them to the couch in the living room. I was finally able to get them back into their own bed on a regular basis after four months.

For weeks following Jerry's death, I lived in shock. When that began to wear off, I fell into an emotional black hole from which I could not escape. I had no desire to live. I hardly cooked any food for months. People were kind, especially at Christmas, but I felt like I was living in a vacuum. When Jerry had been gone six months, I realized I needed to feed my children better; even so, it took conscious effort to cook for them. Three months after Jerry's death, Jessica and Joel went to winter Bible school and we got very lonely while they were gone. I felt like I was losing everyone. It was a long winter. Many times I cried to God, asking for something to fill my need right then. Often He gave me a specific Scripture to read that would be just what I needed at the moment. Sometimes it was a whole chapter, and sometimes a verse or two. Later I wished I had written down the references but I didn't think of it at the time.

I missed Jerry terribly. We had grown up together and had been childhood sweethearts. We were just two-and-one-half weeks from celebrating our 20th wedding anniversary when he died. He had planned a surprise for me for that anniversary, but I will never know what it was.

Ron Bear had been working for Jerry and he continued to help me by running our business for a while. He probably is not even aware of the many ways he helped me. The people at the bank were very kind also. They went far beyond the call of duty to help me. I had never balanced a checkbook before, and they were very patient with me. People were kind to us in many different ways. I cannot imagine how we would have made it without friends from near and far to show us they cared, even if they did not understand.

My parents, Robert and Cretora Hilty, have done very much for us. They have been here for us anytime we have needed help with anything. Pop has taught the boys things they need to know and cannot learn from Jerry. He willingly lends his "man power" when we can't handle a job. Mom has kept the children for me many times when I have had to be gone from home. She pulls more chairs up to the table and invites us to eat with them when she knows I am too tired to cook. They have gone far beyond the second mile to help us.

It has been four-and-one-half years now that Jerry is gone, and we have adjusted as well as we can to life without him. I have done things I wouldn't have done when he was here, and did not think I could do—like buying and selling cars—but when faced with no other choice, I found a way to do them. I wish Jerry was here to see how much the children have grown and matured. I wish I could hear his voice and see his smile. I miss my best friend and wish many times he was here to give support and advice, but we have good friends, and God is still faithful.

"But they that wait upon the Lord shall renew their strength; they shall mount up with wings as eagles; they shall run, and not be weary; and they shall walk, and not faint" (Isaiah 40:31).

—*Susan Hoover*
Elida, Ohio

ELMER EBERLY

May 2, 1958 to August 24, 1984

In Loving Memory of Elmer
Sandra (Eberly) Eberly, Wife

Time passes and we proceed,
Our loss still felt, and too, our need.
The emptiness is never filled,
But we accept what God has willed.

To wish him back, we never could,
Our loss is his eternal good.
Although the way looks dark to me,
With God to guide, we need not see.

It's my desire that his passing would
Also be for others' eternal good.
It's worth it all if others can learn
By his sudden death their sins to spurn.

And if by our loss, others can see
The blessing of a complete family,
And live each day in the fear of the Lord
Following the guidelines set forth in His
                                    Word;

Then we'll rest in faith that it's not in vain,
Looking to the day when God makes it plain,
We'll bear our loss and pray that we
Will be reunited forever in eternity.

-Sandra Eberly, August 1985

Elmer died from head injuries while repairing his skid steer.

He left many memories of family life. And his love for singing was an inspiration to those around him.

Elmer left behind his wife, Sandra; one daughter, Audrey (two-and-one-half); and one son, Alfred (one-and-one-half). Several months later, on November 20, another son, Anthony, was born.

Anthony, whom Elmer never saw on this earth, has now gone to be with the Lord. His life was snatched away on January 17, 2001 at the age of 16 years due to snowmobile injuries.

Sandra remarried to Mark Eberly, Elmer's brother, on May 28, 1988. To this union were born one son and four daughters.

(On their wedding day, Carl Martin of the same congregation was electrocuted, leaving a family of, his wife and seven children.)

In the past several years Sandra has been afflicted with Multiple Sclerosis, and accepts her lot in life patiently.

In all this, God has been so good.

Our life is like a poem
We're writing every day,
And many kinds of verses
Are lived along the way.

We often meet some trials
However great or small,
It depends how we meet them
How short they seem or tall.

If we are ever weary
Of walking on this road,
Remember, there's a Saviour
Who'll help us bear the load.

Our life is like a ladder
We're climbing every day,
And when we get to Heaven
Happiness comes to <u>*stay*</u>*.*

-Anthony Dale Eberly, (Grade 8)

Lydia (Horst) Martin

February 20, 1951 to February 7, 1998 (46 years)

In Thy Presence Is Fullness Of Joy
Rhonda & Marla Martin, Daughters

Our family shared many happy moments together... Playing, laughing, taking trips, visiting family and friends, and dreaming of goals for the future days. We were richly blest. Little were we aware of the dark clouds hovering over our lives.

Dad and Mom's life together started October 8, 1977. After a trip to the New England States, they settled into a cozy apartment in New Springfield, Ohio. A couple months later they bought a place in the country near Columbiana, Ohio. In the next six years, God blessed their home with three daughters: Rhonda, Marla, and Amy. Five years later two sons, Curvin and Aaron were added in a two-year span. Life moved along at a normal pace with many activities.

Then Mom was inflicted with six cases of bladder infection in two years' time. After a hard case in February of 1997, then two more rounds of infection, the nurse said she wants Mom to go to a urologist with the next infection. The urologist ordered a kidney dye test, and it came back clear. Mom didn't have the normal energy she longed for. She tired very easily, and it took her a long time to do her favorite things. She forced herself to do her normal family duties, and to take part in church activities. Finally, June 18, 1997, she had a thorough checkup. They also took blood tests, trying to discover what was ailing dear Mom. The test showed borderline for anemia, but another blood count was good. The nurse told her not to worry. But Mom wasn't home long until the phone rang. "We need to do more blood tests," they said. When they called with this report, it was partially good news—there was no leukemia. Mom was referred to a blood specialist at the hospital.

On the 25th of June, she had the first appointment with this doctor. He ordered a CAT scan of Mom's chest, abdomen, and pelvic area. We received the results the beginning of July. The heartrending news was she had lesions on her liver.

Friends were praying for us and encouraging us. Our minds were filled with questions. This happens to other people, but now it was us, too. The doctor ordered a biopsy. In less than one week they confirmed the results of cancer in her liver. Our dear Mom had the dreaded disease.

After much prayer, Mom requested to be anointed. This was a special time for us as a family, sharing this resigning of our will to God's will for our lives, especially as it related to Mom's health. Her resignation to God's will was evident in her prayer that "whatever way brings Him the most honor and glory." This brought a restful atmosphere to her, and to our home.

Our doctor didn't give us much hope with this kind of cancer. Even though he wanted to begin chemotherapy, Mom decided against this treatment. She preferred trying some herbal, alternative treatments.

Toward the end of July, we took a trip to Michigan and Wisconsin. We had a family day on Mackinac Island, and then went to Uncle Gene's in Wisconsin. All of Mom's sisters, (except Janet who was living in Guatemala), got together there.

In August, Mom started having pain in her shoulder and neck. The chiropractor did not want to treat her since the pain was a result of the cancer.

In October, Grandma Horst passed away suddenly. This was a shock to the whole family, and especially to Mom. Her health seemed to take another step downward, which alarmed us. After some more praying and researching, we decided to take ultraviolet blood irradiation therapy (Photoluminescence). This required traveling to Washington D. C. Mom took a total of seven treatments. Immediately after each treatment her cheeks were turned a rosy, healthy color, and our hopes would soar high. But with all the traveling, she developed a stiff neck from sleeping crooked, and that never completely left her.

In December, Mom and her sisters went through Grandma's things. The sisters enjoyed being together, and sharing special memories, but it made Mom tired. She was working on a special project—to surprise her nieces Carolina, Rhoda, and Esther Pichiya of Guatemala with dresses like as she had made for Rhonda and Marla. In spite of not feeling well, she tried to stay occupied with embroidery when she wasn't resting.

By this time Mom's body had started retaining fluid. So she would go to the hospital to have it removed. She would also visit the chiropractor trying to find relief for her back and neck pain. We as a family didn't hear about, or know how much she endured. Once after a friend called, she said, "I'd rather hear about what's going on in their lives than to say how I'm feeling."

Close to Christmas Mom started a nutritional program, hoping to improve her declining health. At times when she seemed worse we would gather in the living room for special prayer—to let our tears flow—and our hearts cried to God for His healing hand. Dad would tell us, "God will heal Mom, if not on this earth, He will in heaven." Oh, how we hoped and prayed that she could remain with us here. At one of these times, she requested not to be taken all over to try to find a 'cure,' because our life here on earth is to prepare for our final home in heaven. Dad took this hard because he was wanting to do all he could to help Mom.

A hospital bed became part of our furniture. Sleeping at night was like "playing musical chairs" (as Mom called it). She went from their bed to the recliner, and then to the hospital bed, while simply trying to find a comfortable position. Aunt Margie started to come at night every once in a while so Dad could sleep. Gradually we became aware of how unsteady she was on her feet. Someone was nearby to give her a hand when she wanted to walk, until finally the day came when she was too weak to walk. Those next few days were full of learning. A lady from Hospice came and taught us some techniques of caring for a bedfast individual. We wanted to care for Mom at home, and she wanted to be at home. She was bedfast the last two weeks of her life.

With the housework, caring for Mom, keeping after our bulk food store, and Marla still being in school, we needed someone to help us. Our cousin Dorene came to our aid.

Mom slept a lot. In between we would visit, read the Bible, the mail she received, or the newly published book, Grace Enough. Friends would stop in and help at night. We would give her wheelchair rides around the house.

One day we took her outside on the front porch, and Marla brought her cats to show to Mom. Though cats were not her favorites, they brought a smile to her face.

Mom took a sharp turn for the worse one Friday night, and till the next night she was in a coma. But Monday she came out of the coma with a cheery smile, and our spirits lifted.

"Rhonda," Dad called urgently. It was early Wednesday morning. "Mom's in a coma again, and is finding it difficult to breathe." Quickly we all came to her bedside. We sang songs of heaven to her, kissed her, and told her good-by. Later in the day she started responding again.

It had been a good while since Rhonda had been to church, and she was considering going to prayer meeting that night. But she wanted to be home if Mom got worse. So she asked, "Mom, should I go to church tonight?"

"By all means," she answered in her slow voice. We chuckled at Mom's expression, which sounded so much like herself.

That night she slept very little. She wanted to go back to the sewing room, and then out to the refrigerator. She thought she could walk if Rachel (a church sister) would hold her hand. She wanted to call her sister Margie on the phone, too. In her mind she thought she could get around, but when it came to the actual act, she didn't have the strength to walk.

By Thursday night she started going into a coma again, and gave evidence of having pain. So we gave her some morphine, which relieved the pain. All day Friday, we had little response from her. We sat by her bedside, doing anything we could to make her comfortable.

Saturday, February 7, 1998 was a beautiful day. Shortly after breakfast, we were summoned quickly to her bedside once again. With kisses and tears showered on her, Mom peacefully joined those that are in the heavenly city.

In Memory
Lloyd Martin, Husband

Losing a companion is a dramatic experience, an experience I would not wish on anyone. Most generally, we may all face this experience in life, some of us earlier in life than others. No matter what stage in life we face this, God's grace is sufficient for each step of the way. We look to the future, and it looks *hard*, but God says, "My grace is sufficient for thee," for this day. We only live today, one day at a time.

I really appreciated the times when someone would ask, "How is it going?" My first thought was, "Do you really have time to listen?" To be able to share my struggle through this experience was one part of the healing process.

One of the many challenges of parenting alone, was meeting the varied needs of my children. The times we shared together in reminiscing of past years were necessary, not only for the healing process in the older three girls (ages 19, 16, and 13 years), but so the two younger boys (ages eight and six years) would at least retain a few memories of their mother. My prayer to God for each of my children, and all those whom He calls to go through similar experiences, is that they may find God's grace sufficient for each day in life.

—Lloyd Martin
Columbiana, Ohio

Nearly two years after Lydia's death, and seven after Myron's, we responded to our own, and our families' needs, and after several months of a family courtship, we married, and joined families on November 6, 1999.

Lloyd & Lorene Martin
(Lorene's story is on page 246)

MYRON M. MARTIN
March 6, 1958 to October 6, 1992 (34 years)

His Mercy Endureth Forever
Lorene (Martin) Martin, Wife

Our life together began in June of 1980. Myron, the son of Ivan Z. and Esther Martin, was a very fine young man, an extra special person. His strength of character gave our marriage real stability.

We had two-and-one-half years of "freedom" before the storm broke over our home. The Lord had blessed us with a sturdy little son, and we were anxiously awaiting the birth of what would be our second son. The clouds gathered gradually. Myron got a very severe pain in his left knee. This lasted a few days, and happened several times over the next year, only seeming to get worse. Our family doctor supposed it to be arthritis, and we focused on controlling the pain.

Finally, with an extra severe case, he asked our chiropractor for an X-ray. They could immediately see what it likely was, and sent him to a bone specialist for a whole round of tests. It was the end of November 1983, when we finally realized the fury of the storm over us.

Myron's faith in God was beautiful, which was my strength in coping with a diagnosis of bone cancer, or in medical terms, Ewings Sarcoma. The relentlessness of cancer makes any decisions for treatment frighteningly urgent. Myron did not make his decision under pressure.

He needed to be comfortable about what he was doing, and trusted God to lead us according to His will, which He did. As we searched the options, we felt comfortable with a doctor who would use the normal treatments in a less radical way.

By mid-December, he had begun his radiation treatments, and his low dose chemotherapy. The doctor assured us that all was progressing well, so it was a shock in July to be told that the area of cancer-infected bone in his knee was actually getting larger. After that Myron always requested a personal copy of any test reports. He began a much stronger dose of chemotherapy, and the remaining ache disappeared.

While we were pleased with this response, we realized there was only so much chemotherapy he could safely be given, so at the prompting of a friend, we looked into alternate cancer treatment, and decided to try therapy of the immune system at a hospital in Mexico. We made our first trip in September of 1984.

This began a series that was to continue for the next six years. He went as often as needed as evidenced by the blood test findings of the health of his immune system, and any returning pain. We went together as a family, and loved the time spent in this easy-going country.

These six years were a special gift from God. The life expectancy of someone with this rare type of cancer is one year. So those ten years Myron was blessed with was a beautiful miracle from God! Four-and one-half years after the birth of our second son, God blessed us with a third tiny, miracle son. And followed with two little daughters. Our hearts flooded with thanksgiving!

But in February 1991, a few months before the birth of our second daughter the X-rays of Myron's knee began to show the cancer area growing again. We found a local oncologist, and Myron began another round of chemo-therapy, and radiation. We continued also with his "immunal" therapy in Mexico, and there found that the cancer had spread to his lymph system.

This downward process only accelerated in November of 1991 when Myron's weakened knee broke. We fully expected amputation then, but the doctors instead all advised to simply insert a rod into the bone, and assured us that his bone was healthy enough to heal. It did heal, but the cancer was growing so rapidly that his leg became immobile.

The next few months brought one heartache after another. A severe pain developed in his hip and a large cancerous mass was discovered. With that came the hardest news to bear. His cancer had also metastasized in his lungs, and we realized that his days were numbered.

But there was more pain ahead. Yet this most fright-ening change in our lives proved to be our greatest blessing! After a growing pain in his shoulder, and weakness in his hand, the doctor ordered an MRI, and discovered a tumor wrapped around his spinal column at the base of his neck. Within hours after we got this diagnosis, paralysis overcame Myron's body, and till the radiation brought it to a stop, he had lost feeling and control from his chest down.

Life changed drastically that April day, but Myron was so thankful for the relief this gave him following several months of severe pain. He took a one week crash course on rehabilitation at Hershey, Pennsylvania. We both had a lot to learn before I would be able to care for Myron by myself.

The next months were busy ones and much more pleasant then the pain ridden ones had been. But Myron's health continued to decline. Since he was paralyzed, we really didn't know what all was happening inside. The doctor limited treatment to only focusing on what would keep Myron comfortable. In September, he was in the hospital again to have fluid suctioned out. We knew the end was nearer.

It was the first weekend of October when his breathing again became difficult, and an X-ray showed that the cancer had filled his lungs. Sunday morning we went up to the hospital for more breathing help, and as he relaxed, his sleep deepened. Friends and family surrounded us the next few days. It was early on the morning of October 6, 1992 when Myron's spirit took its flight.

Losing a companion to the slow claim of cancer is very devastating. But God was always there with His grace. Myron's strong faith in God, even straight through heavy disappointments, was a very constant encouragement to me. His cheerful acceptance of God's plan for him, helped the rest of us to do the same.

There were a lot of tough days ahead. There's not too much to do to "take away" the pain of grief and loneliness. But leaning heavily on the Lord gave an endurance through the pain, and opened the walk toward healing.

Don't measure life by what you feel at this moment. While some moments really seem to be unbearable, they will ease. Next month, tomorrow, even the next hour, you could feel much more at rest.

While there can be struggles to fit your concepts of God's love and care to the devastation He has allowed in your life, DON'T let your feelings destroy your faith in God. ALL that God said, He is, He really is, and a steady faith in Him will be your single biggest source of healing.

It also helps to unload your thoughts and feelings, although there will not always be someone there for you to do that to. But I found as much release in pouring my pain into a journal as in talking to someone else. Find a safe place to keep your journal, and unload your whole heart there. God can resolve hurts and problems when we are honest with them.

Myron's death left me alone—yet not alone—with our five children. Wendall was only 11, Llewellyn (9), Sanford (5), Rosene (3), and Sharita (15 months) at the time of his death. They were a real blessing to me. Children never take the place of a companion, but they gave me someone to give myself to. Their dependance on me, kept me going. And the innocent joy of children kept the pain from being so oppressive.

There were times that I knew I was unable to be all that my children needed, but I had to allow God to use me as He chose. He promises wisdom, and when I needed practical help, I had kind, supportive family and friends. We don't like to feel like a burden, but God means for us to help each other, so humble yourself, and accept the love and care of others.

Don't lose courage. God CAN use you to lead your children back to Him. Don't drop the values your companion had—God can help you to pass those values on. Even now, after several years of parenting alone, my children are a real source of joy to me. Is it because I know "how to do it?" Never! But I plead God's help, and I endeavor in my humanity, to lead them in the Bible way, and how I thank God for then blessing my efforts! But no matter how my story or anyone else's ends, GOD HAS ALL WE NEED!

—*Lorene (Martin) Martin*
Columbiana, Ohio

Practical Ways to Relate to Widows
Lorene (Martin) Martin

"Pure religion and undefiled before God and the Father is this, to visit the fatherless and widows in their affliction, and to keep himself unspotted from the world" (James 1:27).

I'm supposing the call for this subject is because you have the heart of love this scripture is calling for and you want to obey this command, but would like to know how. It's hard to simply answer that request because our situations are different, and we differ in personality. Maybe I should simply explain what James 1:27 really means, and let you do it, and that may be all you need. But I decided to try to share from my vantage what being a widow is like to help you understand how to relate.

Back to James 1:27, there are two words that give light to what God is asking of us. First the word, visit: Strong's Commentary describes it as 'inspect, to go see'. And "affliction" is defined as "pressures." As I see it, God is telling us to be aggressive in finding ways to relieve widows of some of the pressures of their widowhood.

When God calls to Himself a husband, making that husband's wife a widow, He is placing a difficult calling into her hands. I won't pretend it's not hard, and God Himself knows just how hard it is. I can see how well He knows it when I see the emphasis in His word on being a support to widows.

We often say we only realize the value of something when we lose it. Having been the wife of a husband, I can say that's true even in a marriage. While I really looked up to, and appreciated Myron for what he was, there were also many things I just expected him to be, so didn't fully appreciate his filling those unconscious expectations. In other words we take a lot for granted. So if you are like me, you may not even realize what all a widow lost when she lost her husband. Understanding the full realm of a widow's loss will open your eyes to her needs.

First of all, she lost the person of her husband. And that's her greatest, most painful loss. All the things he was to and for her, are not nearly as important as what he himself was as a person. In my case some of what my husband did for me continues: I still live in the house he provided for me, I still drive his car, my material needs are supplied because of his place in a business, and albeit absent; he will always be the father of my children and me still use the values we shared to raise them. But although I appreciate these things; they can do nothing of giving me him.

I'll go into more detail now on what our husbands were for us and what we lost with him. A very obvious thing is that he was our provider. I often thank God for the way He is caring for me, because to need to put your energies into providing for your family's physical needs is a very heavy responsibility added to the many you already had.

Another loss that is part of the providers' role is someone to relate to the business world. We feel this keenly too, because generally speaking, we women feel so inadequate in the business world. We just don't have an uninvolved, businesslike nature. So when an animal gets sick, or something breaks, or a bill doesn't make sense, or we need to make a business transaction, instead of casually, in a businesslike way simply doing what needs to be done; we fight feelings of "Oh dear, why did this happen?" or "Must I call that mechanic or whatever again?" or "They'll think I don't know what I'm doing." We would not ask to be business women.

Another similar loss is that of our decision maker. Weighing facts in a detached manner, again is not a woman, so any decision that requires weighing facts becomes emotionally involving and thus draining. And if we're not sure how to go about deciding, we're ready targets for doubting decisions after they're made. Also, a woman's nature is more cautious than that of a man, so changes that decisions ask for, loom up big and scary. Even above just making decisions, every little thing that my family does is done either by me or under my direction, and that is wearing!

Our husbands were also our spiritual leaders - the one who decided the course for our family in the grey world of uncertainties. He was the one who had charge of family devotions, and chose what church to be affiliated with. He was the one to evaluate and chart our practices and way of life in light of the Word. He also was the one to represent our feelings and convictions in church decisions. With a Godly husband, all that we as a wife had to do was rest under his direction. How am I to know now that I am directing rightly?

Another thing that we as widows lost is the father of our children. He was the security of the children and the home. He was the authority figure. How many of you have observed that your child responds with deeper respect to your husband's authority then to your own? I, as my children's mother, can be as consistent as I know how, but I will never be their father. Will they still be able to grow up to be respectable adults? He was the one to give the solid, patient love, untaxed by the unrelenting hours of mothering that we are subject to. He was the wise one who knew the truth or untruth on all the questions about the wide world that growing children are able to come up with. He was the one most qualified to reproduce his own strengths and knowledge in his children. And as a fellow parent, he was able to identify where I was weak in child-training. Now who is to show me the character qualities that I am failing to produce in my children?

Our husbands were also our protectors. We hardly noticed the darkness of night when Daddy was home. And who checks into a bang in the night? And who stands strong beside us now when some stranger knocks, or we get a silent phone call?

As women in the home, our husbands were our primary avenues of communication. We found out through them what was happening in the world, the church, and the neighborhood, some things besides the little newsy things that women share. And we also were kept in check by hearing about the lessons of life from a man's more solid way of looking at it. He was the one we unloaded everything to, not just the cares of home-life, but the disturbing things we would hear, and he helped us to see it from the right perspective. If we now relate to only a woman's way of seeing things; think how unsettling life can look—you know how our feelings can swing to extremes! Who is to tell us "Now calm down. It's not that bad"?

Our husbands were our companions—the one we experienced life with. Who will share the joys of life with me, or the poignant, precious experiences of my children? I can tell others, but who will feel the joy I feel, and pang in sorrow and pain with me?

Our husbands loved us for the persons we were. Do you know how much of your own comfortableness with yourself comes because of your husband's consistent love for you? Whom do we belong to now? Who really cares what kind of person we are? We belonged to our husband and him only. As described in Song of Solomon 8:6, he was our seal and protection. From within the circle of our relationship, there was a safe and legitimate way to relate to other men. Now suddenly, we belong to no one. Losing the sealing relationship of marriage leaves us feeling unprotected and vulnerable. On the other side of the coin, we can also sometimes feel we belong to everyone, because there is more than just our husband now caring for us.

Lastly, our husbands were the one that we devoted our energies to. He was the reason behind almost everything we did. Sure, our heart did belong to the Lord, but as Paul states, a married woman's place *is* to care for the things of her husband. He was the recipient of our love. Now what is the purpose in life? What is the motivation behind our labors? What can we do with the love that as a living person we still possess?

I hope this has given you a better understanding of the all-encompassing loss we experienced when God took our husbands. But does God plan that the widow should be without these blessings and necessities in life? Are our physical needs to go unmet? Are we to have no more direction in decisions, and our life to finally culminate in one big failure? Must the spiritual tones of our homes deteriorate, and our children be sacrificed to the faults of a single parent? Are we now the victim of every danger in life? And must we become dull, unperceiving women? Is there actually now no one to love what I love, and grieve what I grieve? And must I become an insecure, inferior being? Is there no one to receive the warmth of my love? And am I really left with no reason to go on living?

As a widow, I praise God that He does not desire that any of these be true! While He asks me to sacrifice to Him the person of my husband; He has full intentions of adequately filling my every need for a full and rich life. And I can testify for Him that He is well able!

So how can I experience the fullness He has for me? Firstly, and most important, I must realize that God is the ultimate reason behind everything in life. So it is GOD who called me to the life of a widow. And to experience what He has for me, I must surrender to and accept His plan. Accepting His plan includes accepting the way He chooses to fulfil His plan. In other words, as long as I insist that my daughter needs her Daddy, God cannot show me how to be her security. And as long as I bewail that I can't survive without my husband's love, God cannot satisfy me with the warmth of His own love. So again, the ultimate key to fullness of life is to let God be God above our husbands!

With that, I must also be willing to grow up. The world does not revolve around me, and I don't need to expect everyone to do everything that I want them to. The only way to find contentment and satisfaction as a widow, is to lean on God for all my needs. While others can warm my heart with their care, only God can satisfy!

Now in practical ways, how does God do that? And how can you help? I'll simply go back to the losses I shared before, and look at them separately. But don't let this essay make you think you now know how to relate to a widow, and keep you from 'going to see' as James 1:27 states. Remember our needs are different. First was the loss of the person of my husband. As I said before, God does not give that to us in any other way. But He's generous in His comfort and His grace to live without our husband. You can relieve this loss by talking about our husband to us and our children. We love that, and it actually makes him seem nearer.

Secondly, how does God fulfill our physical needs? I shared my own experience. You'd be surprised at how many of my widow friends are continuing to run their husband's farm. That is no easy task for women, and they will appreciate help and support. There are a lot of ways to help here in the physical labors of the property. Fix their equipment, step in during a rush season (and if you don't know when that is, go and ask as our verse in James says), help in the maintenance of the place before it reaches emergency condition, help with the yard and landscape work. For example: this spring the work needed in my flower beds and around the house looked depressingly monumental. When our minister found that out through a few simple questions, he started a process of action that when I got home from a service the next evening, the work was completely done!

I suppose a lot of these suggestions sound like a man's work, and I share with you as women. Then go as a family to help. But actually, if the widow as a woman, needs to do this kind of work every day, I suppose you can a little too. It won't make you less a woman—it hasn't us, although we almost wonder sometimes!

Another widow friend of mine was left with no means of income as her husband had been a teacher. She had three little girls and another one on the way. But she leans on the Lord very directly for help. And a house has been built for her, money comes in from here and there, and the church helps out also. While the scripture gives the responsibility for a widow's support first to her family in 1 Timothy 5, if you see a need, be willing to share.

Next, how does a widow cope with relating to the business world? I've been supported beautifully in this.

I've bought a tiller and mower since Myron is gone, and in those cases, it was some of our family who did the looking, and the evaluating, and even did, or were with me, for the purchase. While we may want to shrink back from the big business world, I also appreciate the times I simply was told what to do, then encouraged to do it myself. It's a healthy exercise to conquer those inadequate feelings, and by God's grace, just do what needs to be done. Try to understand how you would feel in needing to pursue these things alone, and as a couple be there to help either in person, or with sensitive, understanding encouragement.

After this on our list of losses was that of our decision-maker. As the adults responsible for our homes now, God has called us to be the decision makers. In Num. 30:9, He holds the widow accountable for her own decisions. So respect the decision of the widow. She is responsible for making them. But we do feel, oh, so inadequate, and you can be a big help. First, pray for wisdom for us. God has promised to guide, and we have found Him faithful in showing us the way. How important it is for us to wait before Him! Many times He will show us through the advice of someone else. If you sense a widow is relying on your counsel to seek direction from the Lord, and for wisdom in this complex world, be free, with the help of the Lord, to give practical, clear direction. But if the widow has not asked for your counsel—don't be too free with your advice. It can be very confusing to hear too many sides. If you know of a decision pending and you feel you can be of help, consider speaking to one that she trusts. And if you realize your widow friend has no one she depends on, do assure her that you would be glad to help, but then let it rest.

How can you relieve the weight of responsibility? For one thing, be sure that any help you give truly does relieve the weight, and is not just an exchange of responsibilities. And respect her if she doesn't take on a project that you think would add interest to her life. She just might have enough "interesting" things hanging on her shoulders already!

The next loss is that of our spiritual leader. We lost our visible spiritual leader, but we very definitely still have one in the person of God Himself. I have here a note my husband wrote to be used in his funeral sermon. 'For us to stand in the line of God's blessings, we must be in the line of His commands.' It is very important for the widow to have a close relationship with God, and to spend a lot of time communing with Him through Bible reading and prayer. If God will be faithful in any decision, He will surely be a spiritual one! We can trust Him. A scriptural church is the most restful thing a widow can have. Be a good example to her and her children, and be acquainted with the Word yourselves to have sound advice and encouragement.

Another loss is the father of our children. God is the father of the fatherless as promised in Psalm 68:5. We must rest in His help, and utilize His values of child training, available for the looking into His word. If we do the best we know how, God will add His reward. Not having someone to alert me to my failures is a real concern to me, but even as I lamented that, I remembered the flood of guilt when I'd talked impatiently or been selfish, etc., etc. I do have someone looking on and raising a warning eyebrow when I am not what I should be. And who is more faithful than He to reveal to us our shortsightedness?

Who is the widow's protector? While I still find adult company comforting, I almost have to smile sheepishly at our warped concepts. Who really did protect our family all these years—our husbands or God? How can you help? If you live nearby, be alert to abnormalities and problems, and you really don't have to tell us every distressing story you hear. Instead, share your answers to prayer. And most important of all is, pray for us, for our safety, and for strength to face any dangers that will come. And if you are ever needed in an emergency, please respond quickly, and with kind willingness.

Next is our need for fellowship. God wants us to come and tell Him about our life—He really does care. But He did make us social beings, and He wants to 'set the solitary in families.' I thank God more than ever for church, family, friends, and also for the telephone and mailbox! But I was impressed with the warning for young widows especially in 1 Timothy 5:13 to not be gadding about gossiping. We are not to allow our loneliness to make us mindful of everyone else's business, but on the positive side, how special it is to be able to share with each other. We have remained in a social world, but we do now miss our husband's way of looking at things. So the next time your husband or teenager tells you a special piece of news, think about the widow and the fact that there may be no one coming home and sharing. Help her to feel she is still an acquainted part of the church, family, and community. And when you share frustrations, share also the solid encouragement your husband gave you, so she can benefit from it, too.

Sometimes when she is present, choose to have the brothers and sisters visit together so she can benefit from a Christian man's perspective of life. Visit her as a family—not only when your husband is away (although that's an excellent time for close sharing). Let her enjoy normal family sharing too, and her children relate to 'whole' families. If you would find it more comfortable, or just to add to the visit, bring another family along, to all visit together. Everyone will enjoy the extended fellowship.

Now to the loss of our companion—the one who shared with us the same experiences in life, we say joys are multiplied, and sorrows divided when shared. So extend your heart in interest to the cares of the widow. Several years ago my mother had picked up a food processor free, thinking Myron could fix it. Well, he never found time, and it remained untouched in a corner of my basement. Recently I thought about it, and decided I'd stored it long enough, so brought it up to return to my mother. My sons immediately got interested and had to check it out, and in just a few minutes it was running. Now I feel like telling the world (and obviously am)! Is that desire to share because I want you to know how smart my son is? Not necessarily, but because he's showing special traits of his Daddy, and his Daddy isn't here to enjoy that accomplishment with me. Understand the need to share, and take a sincere interest in the family and their interests.

Our next loss is the love of our husbands. Is it true that we are no longer loved and enjoyed by anyone? I was thinking those thoughts in my working through Myron's death, and the Lord let me know plainly that He loves me in a special way. And my defeats are His losses, and my growth is personally enjoyed by Him. I do belong to Someone, and that Someone really cares for me. We can argue that's not what we meant, but we must remember—to receive God's blessings we must allow Him the right to choose how He'll give them. We can pursue life with the value of what we do, coming from the love and acceptance of the One we personally belong to. Your love, acceptance and support can reinforce our continued worth as a person, too. And how are we to relate to the loss of the seal of our relationship with our husband? The Bible gives direction for all women to possess a meek and quiet spirit, and an extra reserve on the part of the widow can simply be our protection from relating too loosely.

Lastly, we deal with losing our purpose for life. We do not become restless because we lack work to do, but because that work loses the purpose it used to have. As a young widow I have my children to work for, but admit it, we were used to more than that. I have to think again of 1 Timothy 5:11. It is stated plainly there that as a young widow, I am not to look around me for fulfillment of my needs. I am to allow my needs to drive me to God, because it is only while leaning on Him that I will find any satisfaction in life. He knows that we tend to come only as close to Him as we feel the need to. But if we look elsewhere in our emptiness and heart cries, our back will be to Him, and we won't see His arms extended to us and all the gifts of love He has for us. Then NOTHING will satisfy the restlessness within our hearts. But while we purposefully occupy ourselves with searching out the Lord, and consciously rejoice in the many blessings in life that He has given us, we will find that to be purpose enough. When I am willing to devote the energies of my love to Him, my heart won't be groping and broken. What can you do? Again pray for us. Pray that God will light our way with purpose. Pray that He will give us grace to rejoice in Him. Pray it again, and again.

I hope that you can see better the inside life of widows and realize that while our most intimate relationship has changed to a spiritual walk instead of a physical one, we are none the less well-provided for. Let this propel you up from a seat of pity and into an active role of help and encouragement.

You may be thinking that you have tried to help someone and they didn't seem as grateful for it as you thought they would, or maybe they didn't even accept your help. We happen to have some inside battles when we receive help that affects our reactions. First of all, it is very hard to ask for help over and over again. We like the open offers for help, and the times someone said, "I want to come next week. Do you have a list of things I can do?" Another thing we must work through is, "Why must others be doing this instead of my husband?" But I can thank God that others are doing it instead of me needing to, or worse yet it going undone. Another reaction is, "Everyone is so busy, and needing to help me will strain our relationships." It's true, most everyone is busy, and thus I will do what I can. But I must remember that my husband was a busy person, too, and I accepted his help. Yes, I could because I knew he loved me and wanted to help. But can I accept that others just might love me, too, and really want to help in spite of their busy schedules?

And lastly, I may cry "I want my husband, not a letter, or meal, or money, etc., etc." No, you cannot meet my true heart cry, but what you do for me is special too, and most important, it represents your love and care, and I can choose to gratefully accept your care in whatever form it comes.

Finally, the Lord calls us to be strong, and grow up in Him. We try—we work hard, yet we also remain human, like everyone else. So pray for us, encourage us, and lend a hand. We really appreciate your love and would never want to be without it!

"But I rejoiced in the Lord greatly, that now at last your care of me hath flourished again; wherein ye were also careful, but ye lacked opportunity. Not that I speak in respect of want: for I have learned, in whatsoever state I am, therewith to be content. I know both how to be abased, and I know how to abound: every where and in all things I am instructed both to be full and to be hungry, both to abound and to suffer need. I can do all things through Christ which strengtheneth me. Notwithstanding ye have well done, that ye did communicate with my affliction" (Philippians 4:10-14).

Lorene (Martin) Martin
Columbiana, Ohio

Contributors

C380

Contributors